D1827270

ESP
AND
Dream
ANALYSIS

ESP
AND
Dream
ANALYSIS

Katharine Cover Sabin

HENRY REGNERY COMPANY
CHICAGO

Library of Congress Cataloging in Publication Data

Sabin, Katharine Cover, 1910–
    ESP and dream analysis.

    1. Dreams.   2. Extrasensory perception.   I. Title.
BF1078.S16   133.8   74-7072
ISBN 0-8092-8397-2

Copyright © 1974 by Katharine Cover Sabin
All rights reserved
Published by Henry Regnery Company
114 West Illinois Street, Chicago, Illinois 60610
Manufactured in the United States of America
Library of Congress Catalog Card Number: 74-7072
International Standard Book Number: 0-8092-8397-2

Contents

Preface

Any person who claims a breakthrough in ESP—especially a breakthrough of such magnitude that many average people are enabled to foresee future events—should offer proof.

For the past five years I have been establishing the value of my ESP discoveries through the following methods:

1.   By issuing national and international predictions that are the most closely monitored against fraud in the history of parapsychology. These predictions have been proven true with a high ratio of accuracy that defies chance averages.

2.   By teaching my techniques to reporters who then write articles attesting to the fact that they learned how to make predictions on the personal and even national and international levels.

3.   By writing books and courses that allow both the lay person and the scientist to experiment with my methodologies.

A complex set of circumstances has made it possible for

me, a lay person, to arrive at the door of applied parapsychology systems ahead of degreed professionals. It is only
recently that parapsychology has been recognized as a bona
fide science in America; and prior to this recognition, there
were few career opportunities open in this field.

Only a handful of accredited scientists, among whom were
Dr. J. B. Rhine and his wife, Dr. Louisa Rhine, dared risk
their financial future and their reputations by exploring the
possibilities of ESP. Even now that parapsychology has been
admitted into the hall of science, grants and endowments are
inadequate to the cause. Qualified Ph.Ds versed in cultural
anthropology, psychology, as well as many other disciplines,
must, like other people, earn a living and support families.
Few of the scientists who have an intense interest can afford a
full allotment of their time to parapsychology but must make
it a sideline.

I have no degrees, but I do have eighteen hours a day to
devote to parapsychology. This advantage of time allows me to
experiment as I see fit. And whereas academic scientists have
to proceed cautiously in accord with strict scientific protocol—for instance, the Rhines' having to establish ESP as a
fact of life by collecting data and classifying its various
phenomena—I have been free to specialize in promising
areas, giving creativity free rein.

I did have to pause in my research long enough to become
well read in psychology, for psychology and parapsychology
are twin stars, each one shedding light on the other. For
instance, in order to give a full understanding of the way ESP
operates in dreams, I must touch lightly—and I hope most
interestingly—on the differences between Freudian and
Jungian theory.

Needless to say, my qualifications in the area of dreams are
not in the context of a formal education. But as matters stand
today, the science of psychology cannot point to a single
person, no matter how many degrees he may possess, and
proclaim him an absolute authority on dreams. Psychology

has reached the state of being very helpful to humanity, but it is still too young to be unified on all issues. There is no agreement as to the mechanism, purpose, and interpretation of dreams. Freud's dream theories were at once challenged by Jung and Adler, and today it is still the fashion among psychologists to offer their own versions of dream psychology.

This lack of unity on the subject of dreams is no reflection on the erudition and judgment of those engaged in the psychological disciplines. Such a chaos can exist only because the dream has not been explored in its full potential. It is true that psychologists have discovered ESP in dreams without reaching a state of unity—for example, England's Jan Ehrenwald noticed ESP in dreams and concluded that this dimension upholds Freud; whereas, more recently, Dr. Ann Faraday gives the impression that the dream condensation can not accommodate Freudian theory and ESP at the same time. But a mere observation of ESP in dreams does not constitute an applied parapsychology—the only vantage point that can offer a total perspective.

This vantage point offers a surprise, a unification of dream psychology in which the theories of Freud, Jung, and to a lesser extent Adler, join hands—Freud being basically correct and Jung and Adler making contributions that are sound in areas in which Freud is not disputed. For instance, Freud's theories of wish fulfillment, the censor, and displaced people in dreams are challenged by many modern psychologists; but as this book will illustrate, ESP makes the roles of these dream factors unmistakable.

But my main hope for this book is not as a contribution to the field of psychology. It is my wish that individuals in all walks of life will learn to receive guidance and to foresee the future through their dreams so that they may receive greater material and spiritual blessings.

Katharine Cover Sabin

ESP
AND
Dream
ANALYSIS

An Introduction to Dream Control

Go ahead! Here is happiness! Opportunity is knocking! Danger! Be careful! Beware!

How often do such messages flash through our dreams? But we do not heed this guidance, for we have ceased to depend upon the leading of our intuition. Instead, we awake with no memory of our dreams (a situation this book will endeavor to correct), or we can discern nothing in these nocturnal visions except meaningless nonsense.

It is the mission of this book that *intuition*, speaking to us in our dreams, shall be heard and understood. In the history, or the allegory, of Adam—it does not matter which viewpoint you entertain—Adam walked and talked with his God. When we learn how to do this again, our steps will be directed toward paradise on earth.

There are two keys to guidance through our dreams. Paradoxically, these keys are named *faith* and *science*. This book is a meeting ground between religion and psychology. The Biblical claim of dream guidance is true, but not in the sense of a God speaking personally to each dreamer. Instead, our dream instruction is sealed through natural laws operating in man and his environment. As for Freud, his scientific dream findings are also true—except for his failure to discover *precognition* (the ability to foresee future events) in the dream mechanism.

Although this book is definitely not a psychological text, I shall teach how the causes of the dream, once they have been scientifically isolated, actually aid and abet precognition instead of ruling it out, as many psychologists have thought.

Some of our modern sciences, such as the theory of evolution and psychology, have caused many of us to feel bitterly bereft of the comfort and faith once inspired by the Judeo-Christian religions. But the newer science of parapsychology—especially the field of applied parapsychology in which I am specializing—swings the pendulum back to faith. This science teaches that we all do possess native ESP power that can be controlled to solve our problems and obtain a happier state of existence.

One of the great tragedies of the sixties was the brutal slaying of author Max Wylie's daughter by an unknown psychotic who invaded her New York apartment. In an article written for the *Ladies' Home Journal*, Mr. Wylie deplored the death of this bright and beautiful young woman. After eighteen years of dream research, I am convinced that if the Wylie family had kept a record of their dreams prior to the tragedy, I could study it and point out the many warnings that must have been received.

Then why didn't the Wylie family recognize these warnings? Why don't we receive, forthright and direct, the dream guidance intended for our safety, enlightenment, and profit?

We find the answer in psychological science and become

indebted to Dr. Freud. When we understand the complexity of a dream, we can realize why the precognitive aspects must be searched out. The dream pattern is cut from the cloth of the past, and usually some event from the past forty-eight hours, more or less disguised by other dream functions, becomes apparent under close examination. Inner stimuli such as digestive factors and outer stimuli such as noises also have power to influence the dream. The psychological *wish fulfillment* (to be explained as this book progresses) must usually be accommodated, for it often instigates the dream; and there is also an interplay of other psychological expressions coming from the subconscious mind.

Because of all these factors, as well as the *economy* inherent in the dream, the future is usually revealed only in symbols. We do see the trend of the future, but it is masked and disguised.

It is the purpose of this book to help you rip off this disguise so that you can behold the trends of the future before they materialize in your experience. *When the future is known, you can often accept or bypass it, as you will.* Life is fated, but not irrevocably. There is always more than one possible path of destiny.

But before we can benefit from our dreams, we must understand them well enough to be able to sort out the paranormal value from the psychological factors. This does not mean that you must take a brush-up course in psychology; throughout this book I shall teach by presenting true case histories, and I shall often follow through by analyzing both the psychological and the parapsychological dream content. Like Freud, I must undertake this course at the expense of some embarrassment; for when I reveal my own dreams, my psychology will be laid bare on the dissecting table of scientific research. However, my own dreams and those of my mother are a natural starting point for what I have to teach.

They have a comparative value in exemplifying degrees of dream intuition while they lead up to the subject of this chapter—an introduction to dream control.

My mother was one of the rare, psychically gifted people whose dreams are often realistically true instead of symbolically true. According to her, I announced my coming advent into the world, through a dream, fourteen years before I was born. The dream occurred the night after my mother had visited a Gypsy camp to have her fortune told on her seventeenth birthday. In this dream I appeared to my mother exactly as I was to look at the age of four—with big brown eyes and red-brown hair—and I told her that I was to be her only child to survive infancy. From the standpoint of psychology, this dream was manufactured from the material of the previous day, as is so often the case. There is little doubt that the Gypsy fortune teller had told my mother of a future that included a family. Also, it would not be unusual for a young woman to dream of having a daughter with hair and eyes the color of her own, as was the case with my mother and me, and then to produce such a daughter at a later date. In fact, the wish that triggered this dream is obviously a subconscious desire for self-reproduction. The fact that I was the only child conceived by my mother to survive the fetal stage and early infancy can be attributed to coincidence.

But throughout her life my mother had true dreams that can't be scientifically explained away by today's psychological concepts. Once, when I was small, I was delighted to find a beautiful rosary in a vacant lot. I thought it was a great treasure, worth thousands of dollars. How lovely this fabulous "necklace" would look around my mother's neck! I rushed home, and bidding my mother to close her eyes, I placed the rosary in her outstretched hands.

My mother gasped: "But I have seen this rosary before. You placed it in my hands last night, during a dream!"

Coincidence? Perhaps. But as this book progresses, a collection of realistically true dreams will be presented and analyzed. You will be shown consistent patterns that lead to new scientific postulates concerning the manner in which man's ESP faculty is incorporated in dreams. I can't analyze the rosary dream because it is merely a fragment of a dream that was not fully related to me. However, in later chapters I shall have much to say about the associative material of true dreams.

Some of my mother's dreams had far greater value than that of the rosary—which merely divulged a coming event of little importance—for she was capable of receiving dream guidance of life and death moment. Here is an example:

Once, when my mother became dangerously ill, my father engaged an expensive physician—one who attended the rich and was considered the finest in Denver. He made his diagnosis and declared that only an abdominal operation could save my mother. But that night, in a vision, my non-Catholic mother thought she was visited by St. Stephen, who gave her the following counsel: "No! No! Not Dr. ———. His knife will kill, not heal you." When my mother related this dream, my father called in a second eminent physician, whom I shall call Dr. S. He made an entirely different diagnosis of my mother's illness and advised a totally different operation. That night the dream figure who claimed to be St. Stephen appeared again to my mother and again repeated a warning: "No! No! Not Dr. S.! His knife will kill, not heal you!" My mother refused to have the operation.

The following day a neighborhood physician, Dr. Edwards, who had recently attended me during a case of measles, dropped by to check my hearing. My father asked him to examine my mother.

"A simple case of abscess," pronounced Dr. Edwards. "Yet so large and progressed that I must operate at once. Have the servant prepare your wife. It is fortunate she refused luncheon. She must have no dinner. I'll call the ambulance immediately and operate tonight."

My father was outraged by this third diagnosis: "You Denver quacks are all butchers! I'm going to rush someone in from Chicago." As my father and the doctor argued, my mother fell into a delirious doze. Again she thought she saw St. Stephen and heard his counsel—this time happy and triumphant: "Yes! Yes! Dr. Edwards. His knife will heal, not kill you."

And, indeed, Dr. Edwards was right. Later, we learned that the two other operations that had been proposed could have been fatal.

I have no way of tracing what past association produced St. Stephen in the dream series I have just recounted. However, my mother sometimes designed art for a Catholic cemetery, and this may have influenced the dream. The simple wish was to recover, and it must have triggered deep intuitional processes. Freudians would claim that the latent wish was to receive attention from a superior type of man.

My father and I could only marvel at my mother's guidance dreaming. Once he remarked to me: "It is too bad you don't have your mother's gift for dreaming. She certainly has a rare talent."

Today, I understand why my mother's dream faculty was so well developed. Unknowingly, she took *exercises* that channeled psychic ability into her dreams. My mother's dreams were important to her. She reviewed her dreams as she cooked breakfast, and she always related them when we sat down to eat. And at night, as she prepared for bed, she began to look forward to her dreams, wondering what they would impart.

These same exercises have worked for many of my students, and I think they will work for you. If you consider yourself a nondreamer, looking forward to your dreams when you retire, and endeavoring to remember your dreams when you awake, will do much to induce the faculty when combined with other techniques to be given in this book. If you are already a good dreamer, the techniques under discussion will often make your dreams more meaningful and precognitive. But do not expect results in a day or a week. Development of the dream faculty to peak performance takes from six months to a year.

Much as my father deplored the fact that I did not "dream true," I now know that I did. However, the precognitive material was presented in symbols, as is the case with most nonpsychics. Here is an example that will introduce you to precognitive symbology:

I was an independent, adventure-seeking child born to clucking, over-protective parents. At the age of six I would sometimes spend the money given to me for candy on a stolen street car ride, going a few blocks and then ringing the bell and getting off to walk home filled with the joy of freedom and unsupervised accomplishment. One night, I boarded the forbidden street car in my dreams. I had barely settled in my seat before a ghostly figure sat down beside me and thrust a piece of metal, somewhat like a chisel, through the front of my neck and into my throat. There are several levels of psychology in this dream—the simple wish fulfillment to travel in the street car no doubt masking a more deeply hidden desire to escape from parental observation for the purpose of a typical, childish biopsychological indulgence, against which my mother had always been extremely vigilant. From the psychological standpoint, dreams of street cars, buses, or trains sometimes indicate a subconscious fear of illness; and the children of my day were nightly admonished, erroneously, that incurable disease was the inevitable result of self-exploration. Ghosts in the dreams of children often represent parents—those dimly seen figures that hovered over us in baby-hood. There are even deeper psychological indications, which will be discussed more fully in a coming chapter. At any rate, the entire dream deals with the forbidden and that which has been so repressed that the wish fulfillment dare not be obvious. Even so, the dream censor makes the entire situation unbearably punitive.

Food and drug laws were not strict at that time, and several weeks after this dream I purchased some penny candy, throwing part of it away after I discovered metal wires in it and then eating the rest. Subsequently, I suffered a throat infection that defied diagnosis. A tonsillectomy was to no avail; my throat continued to fester. One morning my father detected a foreign object projecting from a pus pocket. When the doctor applied his tweezers, he removed *an unbelievably long piece of wire* that had become lodged in my throat.

The psychological symbol of a street car pertaining to illness is also used *precognitively* in the dream I have just recounted, and I am sure my subconscious processes were trying to warn me against swallowing the wire, which was symbolized by the metal chisel that was jabbed into my throat.

Here is another dream that has been long remembered because it was so seemingly nonsensical that I resented it, even though I was just a child. However, from the vantage point of the years, I can now discern several levels of ESP provided by just two symbols. In the dream, I was playing with other children half a block away from home when another youngster rushed up to me with the urgent message: "Hurry home, Kay, you have a wonderful visitor. God is at your house and he wants to see you." I rushed home expecting to meet the most beautiful personage that human eyes had ever beheld. You can imagine the letdown when my mother introduced me to a person made up entirely of rusted old tin cans—rusted tin can head, rusted tin can neck, rusted tin can torso and rusted tin can arms, legs, hands and feet—nothing at all but rusted empty old cans. Yet my mother pointed happily to this impossible being and said, "Kay, this is God."

One thing that puzzled me, and helped me to remember the dream, was the fact that I was able to associate the tin cans with the previous day's activities—a childish game of treasure hunting during which I had poked through several boxes of discarded empty tin cans that were behind the woodshed of a neighbor who was slow about taking them to the dump, letting them accumulate rust throughout many rains and snows.

We can interpret the dream as follows: God, in our dreams, is often a father figure, and both the simple and psychological wish fulfillment was that my father wanted to see me. Or, we can interpret the wish fulfillment from the standpoint of Adler and discern the fulfillment of a wish for power and prestige among my playmates, for it was I, not they, whom God wanted to see.

Now, for the precognitive content: When I was in my forties, I was to experience a change in my religious beliefs, leaving the conventional for the metaphysical concepts. At that time, I discarded a belief in an anthropomorphic God and embraced the concept that God is principle, operating through life, love, truth, and intelligence.

Returning to the interpretation of God as a father figure, the dream was a warning about my father's physical condition. The rough Denver winters were particularly hard on my father, and at the time I had the dream he and my mother were considering moving to California. Unfortunately they decided not to do so. A few years later my father died from a lung malady brought on by bouts with pneumonia.

I believe that all families should keep dream records, for I am sure that my mother and father were also experiencing dreams, at that time, that flashed warnings against his exposure to the harsh winter climate, or that pointed the way to California.

There is still a third psychological-parapsychological angle to this dream. When very young, children see their parents as gods, and later feel very disillusioned when the parents fall short of this ideal. Furthermore, as Mark Twain has so humorously noted, teen-agers often go through a phase during which they feel highly superior to their parents. I went through this phase during which my parents, it seemed to me, knew nothing at all. But, like Mark Twain's parents, mine seemed to achieve a remarkable mental growth as time went by. The tin can God predicted my coming attitude that my parents were hopelessly outdated and unknowing.

Now that I hold the keys to precognitive dream interpretation, I realize that *most dreams I can remember from the past had precognitive significance on some level of interpretative possibility*. Also, many of my students now realize that they were often "dreaming true," in the past, without realizing it. Dream symbology is simple to grasp and to apply, and this book will teach *associative symbology* in nearly every chapter.

My paper on dream control was published in 1961 and advertised in *Fate* magazine to give me the advantage of a research among greater numbers of people. One of my principle techniques to influence precognitive dreaming is the simple method of pointing to the solar plexus area while feeding suggestions to the subconscious that dreams are to become more meaningful and precognitive and that dreams of precognitive import are to be remembered upon awakening. When this technique was combined with other methods, which this book will explain, most people who purchased my paper reported good results.

Several years after the publication of my dream paper, Dr. Charles T. Tart, working at Stanford University, reported that he could control dreams by giving "dream suggestions" to hypnotized subjects before they fell asleep. Dr. Tart said the subjects, all college men, were able to wake up by themselves, before or after a dream, depending on their instructions. He also found that some would dream about what they were told to dream about—but always with some embellishment from their own imagination.

At the present time, the method of influencing dreams by hypnosis is being given an extensive laboratory testing by Dr. Montague Ullman and Dr. Stanley Krippner at the Maimonides Medical Center in New York. There, electrodes attached to EEG machines are glued to the heads of sleeping subjects who have been previously given the suggestion to dream about subject matter selected by an agent. When rapid eye movements (REM) set in, the subject is dreaming. The EEG machine is quick to detect these movements, and when they cease, the subject is awakened at once and questioned while he is still able to recall his dream. During early experiments, the agent concentrated on a picture postcard, and it was found that objects on these cards, scenic material, etc., appeared in the dreams of the subjects with a frequency that was well above mere chance averages. Furthermore, there was sometimes telepathic leakage from the agent to the dreamer, and in a few instances this material proved to be precognitive. Today, the suggested material for the sleeping subject is selected by a computer, to insure the tightest possible control conditions.

The parallel dream research that has been conducted by accredited professionals and my own informal but productive efforts prove that both formal and informal research have their own values. The techniques of hypnosis used by the laboratory scientists and my method of autosuggestion make an interesting comparison. Which is the better method for controlled dreaming remains to be seen. But from the standpoint of a practical, applied ESP for individual use, autosuggestion has several advantages: (1) I have discovered that autosuggestion works well with people like myself who are not suggestible enough to be good hypnotic subjects; (2) hypnosis is not always available or advisable; it should be induced only by experts; and (3) we often want answers to questions that we do not wish to discuss with a hypnotist.

Aside from efforts to control dreaming, there is no further analogy between the methods of the laboratory researchers and my own experiments. My approach to an applied ESP via dreams has been a revaluation of divinatory methods that have been relegated to the trash heap of superstition for two reasons:

1.   Because these popular methods of dream divination were not handled scientifically, they were not successful.

2.   Authorities on the human mind, such as Freud, who nevertheless had no knowledge of ESP, attempted to explain why these popular methods were not successful.

But I want to remind you that no system will work when essential components are lacking; nor will a system work if we do not know how to operate it. The dream diviners whom Freud investigated did not engage in the entire science of dream divination, nor did they know how to use the tools of their profession. Nevertheless, Freud marveled that these diviners used his own psychoanalytical techniques that had been handed down from the ancients. While Freud admired the sagacity of the ancients in evolving tools for dream interpretation, he deplored the fact that this scientific approach had been devoted to the futility of prophecy.

The truth is, that Freud had observed the remnants and vestiges of a once great science—the *science of dream divination*. I have reconstructed this science, and it is now my pleasure to give it to the world.

This chapter contains so much information that I shall summarize its salient points:

1.   The psychological dream factors discovered by Freud do not rule out precognition in dreams; instead, the dream psychology often forwards a parapsychological content.

2. Dreams can be realistically true or symbolically true. Gifted psychics are more prone to receive understandable predictive material than nonpsychics, who usually receive dream guidance through symbols. However, both the gifted and the ungifted should make a study of dream symbols, for parapsychological material is most often presented symbolically.

3. The future is not irrevocably fated. When we know the trend of the future, we can often avoid pitfalls or be led to opportunities.

4. Dream control begins by looking forward to dreams and expecting them to be meaningful. All dreams should be reviewed as soon as possible after waking up and at intervals during the day.

5. The novice should begin his system of autosuggestion by pointing to the solar plexus area and addressing the subconscious as follows: "My dreams are becoming progressively more outstanding and predictive. I shall remember my dreams after I wake up." These suggestions should be given at intervals during the day and upon retiring.

2

How to Unlock
the Door to the Future

There are four keys to the parapsychological content of your dreams:

1. Fixed symbols
2. Association
3. The play upon words
4. Arbitrary coding

Fixed Symbols

Freud found that a few *fixed symbols* are common to all dreamers. Many have disagreed with his theory that elongated objects, such as pencils, candles, poles, etc., represent the penis and that round or hollowed out objects such as purses, boats, paper bags, etc., represent the female genitals. This is not a chapter in which I wish to discuss psychology per se, for I have too much concerning parapsychology to teach. However, psychology and parapsychology are so entwined and interrelated in the human psyche that a study of one throws light on the other, as both Freud and Jung observed.

After seventeen years of parapsychological dream interpretation, I am convinced that Freud's fixed symbols operate in our dreams with the exact psychological connotations that he claimed for them. However, at the same time that these symbols express the unconscious wish for a repressed sex desire, they can operate to give guidance or to reveal the future. The following is a case history that gives a clear exemplification of fixed sex symbols carrying out dual purposes of psychological wish fulfillment and guidance counsel.

Beauty operators like to talk about their personal affairs as they groom their clients. A girl, barely eighteen, was no exception. As she wound my hair on curlers, she unwound her life. She was extremely proud of being a virgin, and she thought that the two college girls with whom she shared an apartment were fools who were giving away a woman's most precious possession. She not only had more dates than they, but she also had two suitors pressing for marriage. The only trouble was that she could not choose between them. One young man had been a pleasant and dependable friend for years with a tacit understanding that their romance would lead to a formal engagement and marriage. Then came a dashing newcomer who pressed for immediate marriage, and she was so attracted that she wanted to accept his ardent proposal. However, this greatly distressed her old friend, and his mother championed him by telling the girl that she was violating an obligation and a trust.

At that point in the recitation of her affairs, the little beauty operator was called to the telephone and when she came back, we talked for a time of other matters. But a return to the personal was inevitable, and soon the girl recited a recurring dream that was causing her puzzlement and distress:

The dream always began pleasantly. She would find herself in a Disneyland type setting in which she steered a little motor boat among beautifully colored fountains. She could not see clearly to guide the boat; nevertheless, she very adroitly maneuvered about among the fountains without mishap. Then, the dream culminated in nightmare. A feminine hand grabbed the steering wheel of the little craft, crashing it to splinters against the concrete base of one of the fountains.

The psychology of the dream is obvious. In order to maintain her virginity, the girl has had to repress sex. However, the strong subconscious wish for the breaking of the hymen (the boat) by the penis (the fountain) is accomplished in the dream—but not without being masked in symbols and not without punishment from the dream censor (the conscience or the superego).

The parapsychology of the dream is equally obvious. The girl must use her own judgment. She must not allow her suitor's mother (the feminine hand) to wreck her life.

Sex symbols do not always forward the dream parapsychology in their own connotation as was the case in the dream just recounted. Sometimes sex symbols operate parapsychologically through association, or as a play upon words, or as arbitrary coding. Here is an example in which the fixed sex symbol of the snake (the penis) operates through man's long association with the snake as an enemy to forward the parapsychological content. A man dreamed that he saw a snake coiled among some legal papers. A short time later he was sued, unfairly, for a divorce that ruined him financially. Whenever I dream of a snake biting any portion of my anatomy, I know that my subconscious is flashing a warning of an illness that will affect the bitten area.

How to Use the Key of Association

Freud objected to dream divination because he observed that dreams are structured upon past associations, which he reasoned must preclude any glimpses of the future. But out of the hundreds and even the thousands of associations that we make daily, what determines the selectivity? For instance, why did I dream of the television set last night instead of the clock, or the telephone, or the book that I read? I have come to believe that man's ESP faculty has something to do with this choice. And had it not been Freud's business to make associations with the past, and to direct the dreams of his patients toward the past, so that he might discover the situations that caused their illness, I am sure he would have discovered that the past presents the future in many instances. But Freud objected that even if there were such a thing as dream precognition, the problems involved in deciphering this material would be insurmountable. It was his opinion that any person who attempted to predict the future in the dream content by using the tool of *association*, which was his main technique during psychoanalysis, would have to be impossibly gifted with intuition—an objection that could be made to the use of symbolism for purposes of psychoanalysis!

But let me hasten to enlighten you: There is a simple, clear-cut method by which we can use the tool of associative symbolism on the precognitive level even though we may not be highly intuitive. Psychoanalysts strive first to *associate the dreams of their clients with their problems, responsibilities and goals.* So does the accomplished parapsychologist.

One can demonstrate the simplicity of this technique by a consideration of the Biblical Joseph's interpretation of Pharaoh's dream. As you will recall, Pharaoh dreamed that seven fat cattle came up out of the river and into a meadow. Then, these well-favored cattle were devoured by seven lean, un-favored cattle who came up out of the river. This dream was closely followed by one in which seven good ears of corn appeared on one stalk and then seven thin ears, blasted by the east wind, appeared and devoured the seven good ears.

I have little doubt that when Joseph was called before Pharaoh to interpret this dream he made the following inquiry: *"What was paramount on your mind prior to this dream?"* And it is more likely that Pharaoh replied that he had been going over the accounts of grain and cattle that had been collected as taxes, and that he had been wondering whether he should sell this bounty to surrounding countries or whether he should breed the cattle and store the grain. With a background such as this to relate to Pharaoh's dream, the prediction that seven good productive years would be followed by seven years of famine was simple to achieve.

But let us suppose that Joseph was allowed no knowledge of Pharaoh's thoughts prior to the dream; there are still associative factors connected with Pharaoh by which the prediction could be arrived at without the benefit of superior intuition.

In those days kings were more than figureheads. They judged the people, decided whether to maintain peace or war with surrounding nations, and they administered the national economy. Obviously, Pharaoh's dream refers to the economy of his country (the cattle and the corn). And it is interesting to note how well this dream associates with the meaning of Freud's fixed symbol of water pertaining to birth, for we can extend this meaning to conditions that are to come whenever we see the symbols of these conditions coming up out of water.

Freud's final objection to the theory that association can be used effectively in divining dreams was that dream diviners associate the symbolism of the dreamer with their own past experiences. For this reason every associative interpreter must differ from others, and perhaps only one in a thousand would be correct.

However, the wise dream interpreter—whether he is on the psychological or the parapsychological level—does not associate a dreamer's symbols with his own past experiences. Like the psychoanalyst, he can ask the dreamer what his dream symbols suggest to him, especially in situations where there is no generally accepted meaning. But very often there is a general and widely used association with a symbol, and of course, the wise interpreter gives this preference over a competing individual interpretation of his own.

Here is an imaginary example. Let us say that a certain dream interpreter does not like to use a broom. She prefers to use the vacuum, even in the kitchen, because she thinks brooms create unnecessary dust. Will she tell clients presenting her with dreams about brooms that they will soon be handling a situation in the wrong way? Not if she knows her vocation. She will reason that we use brooms, in the most usual and applicable sense, *to get rid of dirt, to get rid of the unwanted*. This association is so fixed in our consciousness that we have the saying, "*a clean sweep*," that applies to situations in which effective action is taken to remove obstacles, impediments, confusion, opposing people, and so on.

Four years ago, I dreamed that I was standing at the door of our guest bedroom while I used a broom to hold back a large puddle of urine so that it would not flow into the other rooms of the house. Urine has so long been a diagnostic expedient that our first association with it is illness. The only *use* we have for urine is to take it to the physician when we wish to know what ails us. We also associate urine with illness in a second sense—contamination.

A week after I had this dream, my stepfather became so ill that I brought him into my home to care for him. The first step I took was to buy him several pairs of surgical pants to cope with the frequent loss of urine that he was experiencing. Next, I had to set up sanitary measures for the laundry sterilization of these items in order to prevent contamination. I arranged for a physical examination by a physician and then put my patient on a salt-free diet to check the fluid that threatened to surge around his heart and into his lungs. While I could do little for the physical conditions causing the symptoms, I could *hold back* embarrassment, discomfort, and even death for my stepfather. *I got rid of distressing and unwanted conditions.*

Some symbols are universal on the parapsychological level.

As I have already stated, water is a fixed symbol for birth in the Freudian connotation. The disciples of Jung, on the other hand, believe that the sea represents the subconscious. But on the parapsychological level, I find a widespread association that relates to making our way financially; for in the sea there is a fierce, competitive struggle for existence among marine animals. In an old, out-of-print book, Frances G. Wickes, a student of Jung who began her practice as an analytical psychologist in 1925, relates the dream of a young woman faced with the necessity of making her own living after a lifetime of being pampered by wealthy relatives, with the exception of a short interlude during which she had earned a little money and purchased a few objects for herself.

The young dreamer found herself watching a turbulent sea upon which she must venture. Boats were tossing about, some disappearing beneath huge waves. Then she saw a little pink, mug-like boat bobbing about, and a dream voice told her to embark in this craft for it would weather the storm safely. At that point, the dreamer looked closely at the boat and recognized that it was her own tooth mug, which was one of the few possessions she had paid for with money she had earned herself. Both Ms. Wickes and her patient agreed that the dream meant the dreamer could be confident that she could make her own living.

In 1960, I had no knowledge at all of Ms. Wickes and her patient, but note the similarity of my dream and its outcome: I stood just within my house as the angry sea raged right at my doorstep, its huge waves capsizing boats and ships as far as I could see. I turned to my dream companion, a boy of ten, and asked: "Have you ever seen this before? Have you ever seen anything as bad as this?" The little dream boy, who must have represented time, assumed a look and tone of great wisdom as he replied: "Oh, yes. I have seen this before. In fact, I have seen it much worse."

The sea became rougher, and I became more fearful. "I

don't like this," I said to the boy. "My husband is out there. I
am afraid his boat will capsize."

"No," replied the dream boy, "you have nothing to fear.
Your husband is safe in the back room of the house." As he
spoke, the boy pointed down a hallway to a room where I saw
my husband seated at a desk with two men. I joined the group
and watched as the two men chatted amiably with my
husband and smiled as they signed a contract.

At that time we were newcomers to San Diego, which was to
be dubbed, historically, "Recession City" during the early
sixties. Nevertheless, my husband soon found a position with
a firm owned by two partners who so valued his sales ability
that they gave him a better than average contract. There was
no recession for us.

Before leaving this dream, I want to point out another
association that is perhaps universal—home and other buildings (shelter) are symbols of safety. Whenever danger is
glimpsed through a doorway or a window, the dreamer is safe
in a situation affecting others. [The wish underlying this
dream could have been a simple desire to live close to the sea.
From the Freudian standpoint, the wish might have been that
the women (boats and ships) in my husband's business life be
rendered powerless.]

Freud objected to the possibility of divining dreams by
association because most dreams do not have the logical
continuity of Pharaoh's dream and are too hopelessly jumbled
to be deciphered by association. This is true, but did not
Freud meet with the same situation during his psychoanalytic
dream interpretation? Yes! And when he did, he fell back on
two other interpretive techniques: the *fixed symbols* that we
have already discussed and the *play upon words* that will soon
be considered in this chapter. We can do likewise. When one
dream technique is not applicable, we can often resort to
another.

But before I leave the subject of *association* and its relation to continuity, I wish to point out that people do not seek out dream interpreters for every dream. When people submit their dreams to me it is usually because their intuition is telling them that the dream is significant. *And when people are impressed that a dream is highly meaningful, I usually find a sustained, logical continuity.* Another thing that makes my task simple is that people usually reveal conditions relating to the dream; as was the case with the beauty operator and the choice she had to make between two suitors, though she, herself, saw no connection between this situation and her dream until I pointed it out.

Here is a reproduction of a letter, so far as I can remember, that proves that the subconscious sometimes fails to warn through a dream, but does make the dream so impressive that an interpreter will be sought out. Note the continuity of the dream.

Dear Mrs. Sabin:

"I don't know why I am coming to you with this dream. I have no problems and I have never been happier. I never saw my father because my mother left him before I was born and came back here to live with her sister, my darling aunt, with whom she had always been very loving and close. The three of us were the happiest people in the world. Unfortunately, when I grew up, I was swept off my feet by a man and married him. It was awful. Within two weeks I was back home with my mother and my aunt, who welcomed me with open arms. We were more happy than ever. We did everything together— painted together, made music for each other, and went out to fine restaurants and good plays. But the years went by, and one day I found my mother dead in bed. And a few months later, my aunt also slipped away from me. I went to the cemetery every day. It made me sad, but it was better than being with other people.

"But three weeks ago, something wonderful happened. I

found that I could make contact with my mother and my aunt through a Ouija board I thought I would try. I am so happy. I have found my loved ones again; it is just as though they are right with me, and I spend all my leisure hours at the board. But last week I had a dream about my mother and my aunt that puzzles me and stays with me. In this dream I was in my upstairs bedroom, and my mother and my aunt materialized and helped me dress for a party that was going on downstairs. I was so happy that they were there, but the odd thing was they were double. There were two of my mother and two of my aunt. After I was dressed, I went down the main stairs with them to our large reception hall and then to the party that was in progress in the drawing room. But I did not like the people at the party. They were dirty and unkempt. I went back upstairs by myself.

"Mrs. Sabin, do you think this dream means my mother and my aunt will materialize for me? Will this happen twice? Is this why I saw two mothers and two aunts in the dream?"

I could not agree with the dreamer's interpretation at all. I knew, as she did underneath, that the dream was one of great urgency. People who have had a history of sex repression had best not further dissociate the personality by using Ouija boards; the two depictions of the mother and of the aunt definitely signified a splitting of the personality. The three women in this case had lived all their lives in an unsuspected homosexual relationship in which actual sex had been repressed. This latent tendency in the dreamer was expressed by the fact that she allowed her mother and her aunt to dress her, in the dream, and then went down the stairs with them. (One of Freud's fixed symbols is that ascending or descending stairs is a symbol of sex expression.) The dirty, unkempt people at the party represent the "possessing spirits," or the delusion of such entities, that is symptomatic of a situational psychosis.

The only good feature of this dream is the fact that the

dreamer goes back up the stairs; for in the parapsychological connotation, descending stairs always signifies a mistake or adversity, whereas ascending stairs is propitious. But note that the dreamer must go back up the stairs by herself—without the "spirits" of her mother and her aunt. Recovery from the symptoms of possession cannot occur until the use of the Ouija board is dropped. Because I am not a psychiatrist, it was not my place to tell this dreamer that her life has always been abnormal. However, I did warn her that those who repress sex often have unfortunate experiences with the Ouija, and I recommended that she apply for professional help to enable her to get herself into the normal stream of life. I did not hear further from this dreamer, so I suppose she did not like my advice and descended those stairs all the way. If so, I am confident that she was able to climb back up, leaving her tormentors behind her.

The Play upon Words

Another technique that is basic to both psychoanalysis and dream divination is the *play upon words*. Very often, proverbs, slang expressions, folk sayings, and puns have either a psychological or a parapsychological significance, and in some instances this word play functions both psychologically and parapsychologically, as is the case in the following example. A woman was wondering whether or not her young son, who had been quite ill, had reached the point of convalescence at which she could expect more of him and apply more discipline. She dreamed that she was cooking in a restaurant and that a handsome waiter kept calling in orders for *hard-boiled eggs*. When she awoke, she concluded that it was time to become more firm, or hard-boiled, with her son.

It is also interesting to note how well the repressed sex wish fulfillment, signified by the waiter and the eggs, forwards the psychological content. The dreamer was married to a man many years her senior who was no longer capable of sex, thus the dream fulfilled her wish for more children by a younger man.

In the following dream a proverb is employed parapsychologically to give good advice. A man was wondering whether to take an offer for his property or to wait for a better deal. He dreamed that he was again a youth eating Thanksgiving dinner at one table with his mother while his father and his two brothers ate at another table. The father pointed to a roast turkey, which was on the table where the boy was eating with his mother, and called out, "Hand me the bird." This dream was advising the dreamer to take the deal at hand, for "a bird in the hand is worth two in the bush." (The play upon words in this dream has an oedipal connotation that will be discussed in Chapter 7.)

Very often, word play is expressed visually in our dreams instead of audibly. At one time I was hoping that my national and international predictions would be published by newspapers and magazines. When I expressed this wish to a rather jealous acquaintance, she remarked, "Don't you think you are reaching for the moon?" I shrugged and went my way. Several weeks later, I dreamed that two women friends and I were walking toward an outdoor platform where a once-popular male movie star was singing. As we walked, I very nonchalantly held the moon in my hand. Two months from the date of that dream, my predictions were featured in *Fate* magazine. It is interesting to note that the two women friends in the dream may have represented the two months through association with the menstrual cycle (woman=menstrual cycle=one month; two women=two months). From the psychological standpoint, our dreams often hark back to the wishes of a bygone day, and the male movie star in this dream was once a great favorite of mine.

Over the years, a number of other dream interpretations have been resolved by applying the principle of the play upon words. At one time, I wondered why my dreams of a close woman friend always depicted foamy soap suds. In one dream she would be down on her hands and knees scrubbing a floor with suds, and in another she would be swimming in a pool filled with them. I did not realize, at the time, and neither did she, that she was becoming an alcoholic. However, my dreams were trying to tell me. "Suds" is a slang expression for liquor, and the fact that the suds in the dream resembled foam was another indication of liquor; for beer is foamy, and the champagne my friend liked so well is full of bubbles.

The slang expression "hot water," indicative of a person or a situation in trouble, often operates in our dreams; the opposite connotation, cool water, is either propitious or warning us to "cool it" in some situations. A writer dreamed that a certain manuscript was scorching but that she saved it by taking it to the sink and turning on the cold water faucet. Shortly thereafter she made some changes in the manuscript and, as she understood the symbol for cool water in the sense of relieving trouble, she thought that the dream had been predictive and that the matter was finished. However, this woman made her interpretation without knowledge that fire or scorching often associates with anger in the human subconscious. Soon, she disagreed with her editors in an angry manner and lost her contract. The dream was not one of prediction, but of guidance, warning her to cool her temper in an angry situation that would involve her manuscript. (In the psychological sense, a book or a manuscript indicates woman; the scorching, passion; and the subconscious wish for the quenching of this passion is fulfilled by turning on the water faucet, the penis.)

"Blowing hot" has long been a term denoting ardor or approval, and "blowing cold" a lack of interest or disdain. Two men who were friends were both seeking individual contracts with the same firm. In a dream, one of these men found himself standing before a door ("the door of opportunity"), and behind him stood his friend. The door opened and the dreamer eagerly started through it. Unfortunately, he was so repelled by a strong, cold wind that he came back through the door and closed it; then he and his friend left the scene. The dreamer was offered a contract by the firm to which he had applied. Soon, however, he resigned, because of the cold disdain of his immediate superior. The companion in his dream was refused a contract by this same superior.

(Note, the Freudian wish underlying this dream was no doubt the desire to compete successfully for sex. Psychologically, a door represents the female genitals. With some dreamers, the opening of a door means the desire to reenter the protective mother-womb.)

Who has not heard the slang expression "sore" used to denote mingled emotions of anger and hurt feelings? And who has not also heard the expression "sore as a boil"? Whenever I see the dream depiction of a friend or a relative suffering from a boil, I know I must be careful not to offend this person inadvertently. And whenever I dream of a boil appearing on my own anatomy, I know I am soon to be chagrined and hurt by another.

We all know that the expression "life in a goldfish bowl" means a situation in which everything we do is observed and known, even our secrets. A woman student of mine expected a visit from her husband's employer's wife and twenty-year-old daughter on a certain date. Wishing to make a good impression, she began making new drapes and sofa cushions, neglecting her house and herself in the process. She reasoned that there was plenty of time to attend to these matters before her guests arrived. In the midst of the drape making, she dreamed that she was looking at two beautifully colored and frilled fish in a goldfish bowl. The next day she was terribly embarrassed because her guests arrived two days ahead of schedule due to a misunderstanding of dates. Beautifully groomed and dressed for tea, the two women guests (the fancy fish) were no doubt embarrassed themselves, and this may account for the inversion of the dream in which it was they, and not their hostess, who were being observed in the fish bowl. (Years before, the dreamer had been given some goldfish. She wished to buy a rarer species but could not afford to do so. This dream may be a case of simple wish fulfillment with no sex connotations, or there may be an underlying desire for pregnancy which may hark back to a previous time as did the desire to own expensive fish.)

The play upon words is so important to parapsychological dream interpretation that I always advise my students to go to the library and take notes from slang dictionaries and books of folk sayings and proverbs. However, I am happy to state that the verbal exchanges in my dreams, and in the dreams of my students, usually become less enigmatic and more forthright after the psychic exercises to be given in this book have been practiced.

The Master Key to ESP

Arbitrary coding is the master key, the great principle by which the average person, who is not gifted with great psychic ability, can unlock the door to the future as it is portrayed in subconscious productions such as the shuffling of coded cards, Rorschach-type ink blots, and dreams. This principle is so essential to dream divination that the next chapter will be devoted to its history and correct application.

3

The Sense and Nonsense of Popular Dream Books

There is both sense and nonsense in the construction of arbitrary codes in popular dream books. Fortunately, there is usually an adequate amount of sense, and I can tell you how to avoid the nonsense so that you may use these books to your advantage. Freud and other experts on the human mind have objected to popular dream books on the grounds that there is no universal divinatory symbology. One book will tell you that a rose means good health, whereas another will tell you that it stands for romantic love. Perhaps a third dream book, whose author suffers from hay fever, will code this fragrant flower to mean an attractive situation that should be avoided. This inconsistency produces a chaotic situation in which a dreamer presenting his symbols to interpreters using different dream books will receive different predictions about his future and conflicting answers to questions held in mind at the time of the dream.

Yet when a friend, or even a stranger, comes to me with a

dream he feels is more significant than usual, I can often rely on the dream book I happen to be using at the time for at least a part of the interpretation and make a correct prediction or relation to a problem in the dreamer's life. Such experiences make me feel sure that the subconscious mind of the dreamer knows in advance that he will come to me and that it has complete knowledge of the code keys I shall be using. Therefore the subconscious is able to produce a dream in accord with the protocol of my particular interpretive techniques. We can therefore solve the inconsistency of dream books and the lack of a universal divinatory code in two ways: (1) find a good dream interpreter and stay with him instead of consulting several about the same dream; (2) interpret our dreams ourselves from the dream book of our choice.

Today, my own breakthrough discoveries in the field of parapsychology are proving to the world that a universal symbology is not necessary to divination. In fact, an arbitrary coding that is highly functional in the production of messages is the *master key* to methods of applied ESP that anyone can use. By breaking with the more universal, "traditional" divinatory meanings assigned to ordinary playing cards and replacing them with meanings obtained through the principles of probability theory, neural association theory, and even computer techniques, I have raised the parlor game of "fortune telling" with cards to a science.

As it is with the cards, so it is with our dreams, for both are subconscious productions. For instance, when we shuffle the cards, the conscious mind cannot dictate that the two of hearts, the ten of diamonds, and the six of clubs shall appear together when the cards are laid out. It is the subconscious, the matrix of our hunches, that makes this arrangement. If we have coded these cards so that the two of hearts means "happiness," the ten of diamonds means "money," and the six of clubs means "coming in," the subconscious has achieved a message through an arbitrary code—we shall be happy because money is coming to us.

Dreams do not have fixed numbers and depictions of people as is the case with playing cards, but their psychologically produced symbols can be coded arbitrarily so that the dream condensation can accommodate ESP. Fortunately the authors of most popular dream books follow a format in which a single meaning, such as making a new friend, often has more than one symbolic representation. This repetitive coding is in accord with probability theory, giving the subconscious latitude in the expression of commonplace events that are often pertinent to the affairs of life. In building my card codes, I also emphasize repetition of meaning, achieving this accommodation for the law of averages through various card patterns. The relationship between coded card reading and the night dream is so close that in my book, *The Cybernetic ESP Breakthrough*, I have related coded card reading to the mechanism of the dream, isolating factors common to both.

There is still another analogy between card reading and dream divination that is important to this chapter. As is the case with those who come to me for dream interpretations, those who come to me for card readings usually have no conscious knowledge of the code I shall be using—for it is their subconscious minds and not mine that arrange the cards, during the shuffle, into patterns I shall read. In this phenomenon, we have support for my theory that the subconscious minds of those who come to me for dream divination have a thorough knowledge of the arbitrary code I shall be using.

Arbitrary coding is particularly valuable to dream divination for two reasons:

1.   When we interpret our dreams through association

alone, we may set up a psychological block against an unpleasant prediction that it is best for us to know. A fixed, arbitrary coding, on the other hand, gets this message through, and we can take action to avoid or mitigate a foreseen misfortune.

2.   The subconscious must react to psychological and physiological stimuli as well as parapsychological stimuli. It can sometimes perform this threefold mission best by using an arbitrary instead of an associative symbol. Because the dream must perform on several levels, we seldom experience realistically true dreams but must study the symbols for what they are worth as we evaluate them through the techniques of association, arbitrary coding, psychological coding, and the play upon words.

The first step toward using a popular dream book effectively is to choose one that lists many symbols. At the present time, I am using a book titled *Your Horoscope and Your Dreams* that is published by Books, Inc. in New York. When I can't find a symbol listed in this book, I refer to other dream books until I find the symbol I am seeking. Always cooperate with your subconscious mind by referring to your dream books in a prearranged succession. Let us suppose you have a large dream book supplemented by two smaller books, one by author White and one by author Black. Always refer to your large dream book first. If you can't find the symbol you are seeking, then turn to the supplementary book you have previously designated to be your second choice. If you have chosen author White over author Black for a second reference, stay with this arrangement. Do not turn to author White as your second reference one day and to author Black's book the next day. Refer to author Black's book only if you cannot find your symbol in your large dream book or in author White's book. It is necessary to maintain this exact order of reference because author White's book and author Black's book may both contain the symbol you are seeking, yet ascribe different meanings.

After you have your dream books and have trained your subconscious mind to follow them, in accord with instructions to be given later, you will no doubt have an experience analogous to the following imaginary example. You have a dream in which an elephant is sitting in an area of your family room that is usually occupied by your desk. The next morning you remember your dream and eagerly refer to your number one dream book, where you find the following listing:

"*Elephant*: To dream of this animal performing in a circus means that a coming business transaction will be to your advantage."

Because the elephant in your dream was not performing in a circus, you turn to your second dream book which states:

"*Elephant*: When you dream of an elephant eating tall African grass, it will be better to follow the advice of another in an important matter, instead of trusting your own judgment."

The elephant in your dream was not eating tall African grass; so as a last resort, you turn to your third reference book, only to learn that elephants are not listed at all!

Since the nonsense of dreams often depicts life forms or objects in unusual places, it is nonsense for dream books to restrict life forms or other objects to places we expect them to be, or to any other particular place. In the imaginary example of the elephant sitting in your family room, use the meaning given in the first book, and let the elephant stand for a business transaction from which you may benefit.

Another mistake made by popular dream books is the restriction of life forms or objects to specific conditions. Here is an imaginary symbol interpretation that is highly analogous to the nonsense of popular dream books: "To dream of a duchess in her fur-trimmed court cape means that you will become acquainted with an interesting person." Now just how apt is the dream of a duchess to occur to the average person? And if the duchess is restricted to one wearing a fur-trimmed court cape, the odds against dreaming of such a personage are astronomical. If you have dreamed of a duchess at all, even one in a gingham dress that is on backwards or wrong-side out, use the meaning in the dream book, and be prepared to make an interesting new acquaintance. Then, for future reference, revise the meaning in accord with probability theory. Since the average person seldom dreams of a duchess, code her to mean something more important than the commonplace happening of meeting an interesting new acquaintance. Let her stand for a new acquaintance who will become one of your dearest friends. The next time you dream of a duchess, or if someone comes to you with a dream of a duchess, interpret by your revision.

There is another mistake made by popular dream books that is also in conflict with probability theory. An ordinary, often seen object, such as a sandwich, may be given a fabulous meaning such as inheriting a fortune or discovering a payload gold mine! Revise your book to let the sandwich symbol be more commonplace, such as an extra way to earn a little money.

So far in my delineation of dream books, I have discussed only the symbolic values of *objects*. Now it is time to offer a consideration of the symbolic value of *actions*, or dream "verbs." Actions as well as objects can often stand alone to provide a coded message, or interrelate with objects, a function that opens up many circuits for message possibilities. Here is a short arbitrary coding I have made up for an example. The actions are so highly functional that I advise you to revise your number one dream book with these meanings:

Olives: Ripe olives denote past mistakes or indiscretions intruding into the present. Green olives denote temptation. Stuffed olives are a warning not to reveal your secrets.

Eating: Very often, if you eat an object in a dream, the advice, events, or conditions of which the object is a symbol relate particularly to you, the dreamer. However, if another person in the dream does the eating, the portents are for him; but there is a possibility that you will be affected.

Jumping: Jumping up and down in a dream denotes unnecessary worry. If you are worried about a present situation, the next difficulty that crops up in your life will clear. If you jump over an ill-omened object, you will overcome or bypass the predicted evil. If you jump over an object that portends good, you will overcome obstacles standing in the way of this benefit.

Burying: Burying an object in the ground denotes that the person performing this action wishes to hide or cover up whatever condition or event is symbolized by this object.

Now let us suppose you dream your mate is eating stuffed olives. You have been warned to tell him (or her) not to reveal secrets or be too talkative. Perhaps the dream is still more explicit; you see your mate eating olives in a business office. Warn him, or her, not to divulge valuable business secrets. Or let us suppose you dream you are jumping over ripe olives. If you are worried over a past mistake marring the present, forget it. If there is no such worry in your present affairs, the next time such a situation threatens, there will be no bad results. To give another imaginary example, let us say that you have children and that you dream of a group of young people eating green olives. You have received a warning to watch the company your children keep, and you should see that they are well supervised. In still another dream situation, you might find yourself burying ripe olives. This would be a warning to keep a past mistake well hidden or to bury the past and forget it. If you find yourself digging up stuffed olives, you will discover another person's secrets; but if another person is digging up ripe or stuffed olives, take precautions so that your own secrets will not be discovered.

Of course, actions are not restricted to relating only to the objects I have listed above for illustrative purposes. Digging in the ground is, I believe, a universal symbol that indicates delving into the past. Here is one of such dream experiences that occurred to a woman when she was quite young and had broken with an old suitor to marry another with whom she moved to a distant city.

The Buried Corpse Dream. The dreamer found herself digging in the ground in search of she knew not what. She uncovered a bouquet of withered flowers and then dug deeper. To her horror, she dug through the lid of a coffin and beheld the corpse of her old suitor.

A week or so later, when she had to go to town on an errand, she spied her old suitor walking slightly ahead of her on the opposite side of the street. Surmising that he had come to her city for a convention that was then in progress, she made no effort to contact him; she knew he was still in love with her, and she felt it best not to let him know her whereabouts. Years passed, and after the woman became a widow, she returned to her hometown with the intention of looking up the sweetheart with whom she had broken. It was not to be. He was dead. The dream had been a true portent that the old romance was "dead and gone forever."

Occasionally when you refer to your first dream book, you will find a symbol listing that cannot possibly relate to you or your affairs. For example, a stout, sixty-five-year-old woman of my acquaintance had no interest at all in sports and no connections with this field. She dreamed of parsnips, and when she referred to her first dream book found them interpreted as follows: "*Parsnip*: To dream of this vegetable means you will rise to prominence in the field of sports." I tried to make an association between parsnips and her present problem, which was financial, but I could not. I advised her to turn to her second dream book where she found the following meaning: *"Parsnips:* When this vegetable appears in your dreams, it is a sign that your financial condition will be better than it is at present." Of course, I told this woman to rely upon the interpretation in the second dream book. Even if the symbol had not related to a current question (perhaps giving a warning against gossip or some other situation that could logically apply to a woman of her age and station in life), my answer would have been the same—to stay with the meaning in the second book instead of referring to her third book.

In the above example, had a second party appeared in the dream, say a young male grandchild, the prediction given in the first dream book—a rise to prominence in the field of sports—could very well apply to him.

We must always be careful not to pass up a meaning in a dream book and turn to another simply because we do not like the meaning given in the first book. And we must remember that many predictions that may seem very farfetched and improbable often come to pass. The following is an example from my own experience.

The Flea Egg Dream. I dreamed that a friend gave me an appealing kitten. I began to pet it but was shocked to learn that its fur was matted with flea eggs.

I knew that the kitten represented a young person, for cats usually represent people in my dreams. When I looked up the meaning of flea eggs, I could not find them listed, nor could I make an association. However, my dream book did list fleas, stating that they mean the discovery of a "nefarious plot." I could give no credence to this interpretation, for I do not know people who become involved in nefarious plots—or so I thought.

The next day, the sixteen-year-old daughter of one of my friends came to call. Delighted, I produced coke and cookies, for I like young people and this girl had always been charming. You can imagine my shocked surprise when the girl told me that she was so angry with her parents for not letting her use the family car, after she had had an accident, that she was going to slip the car keys to her boyfriend so that he could plunge the vehicle off a cliff that night! Of course, I had to warn the girl's parents against this "nefarious plot"—a deed for which she thanked me after her next birthday. One of the most amazing features of this dream is that the girl's name is *Kitty*!

The above dream reminds me that any time you discover a trend of meanings in your dreams, such as the way cats represent people in my dreams, stay with this interpretation instead of consulting dream books regarding them.

I have a friend, a business woman, who can always rely on her dreams about hair. If she plans to make a certain investment and dreams of blonde hair, all is well. But when she dreams of black hair while contemplating an investment, she is warned against it. A dream of red hair means that time is of the essence and that she had best make the investment before someone else snaps up the deal.

Sometimes the station in life or the occupation of an individual makes it imperative to discount the value given to a symbol or an action in a dream book. For instance, a dream book might state that to dream of a carpenter is the luckiest dream of all. However, this dream can have little value for a person who owns a construction company; for the law of association that operates in dreams is apt to cause him to have more dreams of carpenters than is the norm. If you work in a warehouse and dream of a warehouse, or working in one, try to find an associative meaning regarding your work instead of looking up the arbitrary meaning accorded warehouses in your dream books. If you can't make associations with other symbols in your warehouse dream, then look up these other symbols in your dream book.

Most popular dream books allow a small percentage of depressing or ominous dream symbols to stand for fortunate or happy predictions and a small percentage of pleasant symbols to mean unfortunate events or unhappiness. These opposites are scientific, for when we are ill or depressed, or psychologically reacting to a past trauma, we are quite apt to have frightening or depressing dreams at a time when the subconscious may wish to predict a happy event. On the other hand, when we are well and happy and not reacting to morbid or punitive psychological stimuli, we are apt to have happy dreams just at the time when the subconscious may wish to warn us of an approaching danger. Some of the ancient dream books coded by opposites altogether, but this is an imbalance and unscientific.

Popular dream books of today are usually very wise in coding death dreams—corpses, coffins, cemeteries, etc.— with meanings that predict ordinary or good events; for dreams of death are far too common to be coded as death signs. Occasionally, however, death dreams are true in their own significance. When Abraham Lincoln dreamed that he saw himself lying in state in his coffin, the dream did not mean he would make a second marriage as most of the dream books of his day claimed. He foresaw his own death; for within a short time he was lying in state in his coffin. True dreams, however, are very rare. We usually dream symbolically.

Arbitrarily coded symbols can interrelate with a remarkable continuity as the following dream proves.

The Gingerbread Dream. I dreamed that a large tomcat, which we had at the time, was eager for me to follow him.

How proudly he pranced before me, leading me to a fair where I purchased and ate some gingerbread.

According to the dream book I was following at that time, *Your Horoscope and Your Dreams*, eating gingerbread means an invitation to a wedding. Two weeks later, I was invited to the wedding of a young male friend. As I have stated before, cats often stand for people in my dreams, and the tomcat revealed the sex of the person who wanted me to attend his wedding.

There is still another symbol in this dream, the fair, which *Your Horoscope and Your Dreams* had coded to predict a full enjoyment of life. No one enjoys life more than I, and my young friend has found a great deal of happiness in his marriage. The three arbitrary symbols involved performed in a perfect continuity to predict the future.

Here is a still greater example of the ability of the human subconscious to sustain continuity throughout a dream to predict the future via arbitrarily coded symbols. This dream is all the more remarkable because the dreamer was a woman who had no conscious knowledge whatever of the code keys by which I would interpret.

Although my elderly landlady lived next door to me, we seldom saw each other. She was a socialite with engagements around the clock, whereas I was deeply involved in psychic research. When she developed a painful back ailment, I saw her even less, for she kept to her room. Then one day my phone rang. It was my landlady begging me to come over; she had had a dream she felt was significant. I picked up my dream books and rang the bell next door. My landlord welcomed me and ushered me to his wife's bedside, but she did not relate her dream until her husband had left the room, closing the door behind him as he was bidden. The she began with anxious eagerness.

The Dream of the Seven Roasts. "I did not much like my brother-in-law while he lived, but after he died I felt I had always been too critical of him. So it seems very odd that he appeared in this dream that I am sure has a hidden meaning for me. In the dream, my brother-in-law was dressed in a brown suit—a color he never wore, that I can remember—and he smiled as he placed seven roasting pans, each containing a roast, at my feet. Then he pointed to a high window through which a glorious light began to pour into the room."

Because I had coded brown clothing to denote illness, it occurred to me to ask what disease had caused the death of the brother-in-law.

My landlady's eyes clouded with fright. "Cancer!"—she half-whispered the word.

Then I knew why she had insisted that her husband leave the room. She was afraid that she had cancer of the spine and that this information was being withheld from her.

"You need not worry about cancer," I assured the sick woman. "You will soon resume your seven-day-a-week social life; for according to the dream book I am consulting, roasts mean social engagements. A window offers protection from anything that is seen on the outside, which in your case is a brilliant light representing radiation. Rest assured that you will not have to have radiation therapy. Besides, most dream books code a brilliant light as a good omen."

The predictions I gave my landlady were correct. Soon she was able to resume a full social schedule, which she is still enjoying though nine years have passed since I interpreted her dream.

Full instructions for training the mind to follow codes in dream books will be given in Chapter 12.

Not all dreams have so simple a coded continuity as *The Gingerbread Dream* and *The Dream of the Seven Roasts*. The ESP content of some dreams is wholly dependent upon association, rather than a code. Other dreams are quite complex, combining both coded and associative values. You will be taught the techniques of interpreting these complex dreams in the next chapter.

4

How to Combine
Interpretive Techniques

This chapter is written to give you expertise in selecting and combining two major techniques—*association* and *arbitrary coding*. As the chapter progresses, you will be given a depth understanding of the way these two major laws of ESP interrelate to structure various systems of applied parapsychology that are related to dreams.

One of the first things we must do, when appraising a dream for ESP content, is to decide between the two possibilities listed below:

1.   Is the dream a prediction of a coming event that is not yet within the realm of our experience?

2.   Is the dream a prognostication of a present life situation? Perhaps the answer to a question we have been pondering?

Very often symbols found in a dream book will help us make a proper classification, but at other times we must attempt to decipher through association. And in cases of a complex parapsychological content, we must know how to apply both methods. The art of knowing when to use an arbitrary coding and when to decipher the dream through association, and when and how to combine both methods, is very simple—as simple as common sense.

A study of aboriginal practices reveals that arbitrary coding and the techniques of association are at least as old as the totem pole. Totemism is the belief that a natural object, such as an animal or a plant, will lend its virtues and protection to the individual, family, or tribe associated with it. In return, the selected object is also protected. It is not eaten. It is taboo. More than this, the selected object is deified by the erection of a pole that represents a magical affinity, a polarization of power between totem object and man.

But regardless of superstition, the totem is not without a symbolic value that seems in the category of magic until we become better acquainted with the science of parapsychology. Individuals, families, and tribes come to be identified with their particular totems, and this affords a coded frame of reference for dream divination. Shamans and medicine men who have trained their dream faculties pay particular attention to dreams of totem animals. For instance, if a shaman dreams of a bear that has lost its head, he has an indication that the bear tribe will lose its chief. Or, should he dream of a bear being roasted, he would most likely predict that the village of the bear totem will suffer a fire. In both instances, a set code has been combined with associative processes.

The above examples apply to spontaneous presentations of coming events, but the shaman can also apply the virtues of the totem animals and plants to questions that are put to him. Let us imagine a situation in which a tribal chief might want to know whether or not to open an offensive warfare against a tribe whose totem is the rabbit. The shaman meditates upon the question, gives himself the suggestion to dream true, and beholds the following vision—a tiny rabbit with thumping feet that become gigantic. Because the feet of the rabbit are his defense weapons, the shaman would most likely advise the chief not to attack the rabbit totem tribe. At another time, the chief might want to know whether a move toward the south would produce more food. If, while pondering this question, the shaman were to dream of a raccoon, a totem supposed to be able to supply food for its tribe, the shaman would no doubt report to the chief that food would be plentiful in a southern direction. However, let us suppose the shaman had a dream in which a raccoon began to shrink. He would then know that the contemplated move would not be advisable.

The novice at dream control may not at first enjoy dreams that are so logically interrelated as the imaginary examples given above. In fact, his first dreams may be untrue in regard to the outcome of a situation—perhaps just the reverse as in the following example.

At the time of this dream, I was in a business organization in which my immediate superior was in a power conflict with a man in another department who was trying to have him thrown out of the company. In my dream, the two men were in physical combat, and my superior landed telling blows on his opponent's face. As a result, the opponent's cheeks wrinkled and his hair turned white.

As the situation came to pass in waking life, my superior did not best his opponent. He was cleverly discredited and had to leave the company. However, his opponent had to undertake so much responsibility, due to the change, that he aged rapidly. Three years later, his cheeks had flabbed and wrinkled as I had seen them in my dream and his hair had turned prematurely white.

Although simple wish fulfillment is present in this dream, I am happy to be able to state that it has been my experience and the experience of my students that perseverance in making demands of our dream faculty has altered our dreams for the better. Now we seldom have dreams in which a simple psychological wish fulfillment gives us a wrong lead to the outcome of a future trend that is important to us. A further discussion of handling such simple wish fulfillment will be found in Chapter 6.

There are certain techniques that you can use to train your subconscious to bring your dreams to logical conclusions that will indicate the outcome of events as they are to happen in life. One way is to set up a logical, associative, action-and-condition coding around a chosen symbol. For example, most dream books code a hill or a mountain to represent a task or a project that will entail a great deal of work. We can elaborate upon this symbol and get a great deal more out of dreams in which it appears by converting logical associations into the following code. If we are merely surveying the hill or mountain, the dream indicates that the total task lies ahead of us; it goes without saying that a mountain must represent a much bigger task or project than a hill. But if we are already climbing and can gauge the distance ahead of us, we most likely have been given an indication of how much work lies ahead in a present project. If we turn back before reaching the summit, we have been given an indication that we may leave the work or project unfinished at the dictate of our own volition. However, if some person or force turns us back, or if we fall, we may be forced to leave a task or project because of conditions beyond our control. The ease or difficulty with which we climb are also indicative factors. Even the conditions around a hill or mountain have their own messages. If the weather is clear and bright, we shall no doubt be able to reach the summit without encountering "stormy conditions" or heavy opposition. If a hill or mountain becomes too formidable and craggy at a certain point, we are no doubt receiving advice to leave a project or goal that will be more trouble than it is worth. The most fortunate dream of a mountain or a hill is to reach the summit. According to the law of the *play upon words*, such expressions as "he reached the summit of popularity" or "he reached the summit of his ambition" give us a clear indication of victory and success in a life pursuit.

My own success with the ESP content of dreams was not initially the result of a conscious effort to build up such a logical and scientific code as the above. It was my subconscious, not my conscious mind, that opened the door to dreams as an applied parapsychology. Today, I am convinced that reading the future by my card codes activated associative processes to facilitate the presentation of ESP via my dreams. I am certain, also, that this process helped bring my dreams to meaningful conclusions.

The first dream development that resulted from reading cards was a shift from ephemeral to more substantial portrayals. These ultravivid dreams often produced an emphasis on material pertinent to ESP and a fade-out of material that had no precognitive value. The following is such a dream.

The Attic Dream. I went upstairs to an attic that was filled with the usual discards—a dress form, a baby buggy, old toys, and boxes of shoes and clothing. Suddenly the attic and all its contents, with the exception of a single object, disappeared. All that remained was an old trunk that became more and more outstanding and dimensional as the rest of the dream objects faded.

I am not the type who, by nature, is sensitive to signs and symbols. To me, a rose was a rose was a rose—nothing more and nothing less. I can still remember how bored and contemptuous I once was of any literature that expounded symbolic values. My native ineptness in deciphering signs and symbols is indicative to me that if *I* can learn to interpret on the associative level, everyone can. But I was impressed by the fact that the dream trunk had not faded out along with the rest of the objects in the attic but had become more vivid. I went to the public library and consulted the popular dream books. Many of them didn't give a meaning for a trunk at all. When they did, I was informed that if you packed a trunk, it meant taking a trip; but if you unpacked a trunk, it meant a visitor from a distance. Nothing at all was said about a vision of a closed trunk—they were simply plain old trunks to which nothing was happening.

Then, in less than a month, my husband was faced with a decision. He was offered a position with a new company that would require us to leave the state of Colorado and move to Arizona. The vision of the trunk flashed into my mind, and I knew it was a signal for us to make the move. That was my first lesson in dream association.

Later, when I began to train my mind to follow dream books, I formed the habit of consulting them before attempting to evaluate dream symbols associatively, unless I knew immediately upon waking up that the dream had presented an associative clue to a situation that I could recognize or had answered a question I had in mind. I still follow this regime, and I recommend it to my students. But if I have received an outstanding symbol that I cannot immediately associate with a present condition, and I can't find this symbol listed in my dream books, I review my affairs carefully in an effort to determine whether or not the dream relates to some situation in my life or to some recent question held in my mind. If I can make no meaningful association regarding these matters, I know the symbol must relate to the future. I then keep it in mind so that I can make an association with the predicted event when it occurs.

As an illustration of this principle, I remember an early vivid dream I had of stacks of fresh, clean washcloths and towels. I could not find these items listed in my dream books, and I was so unaccustomed to dream divination that I failed to relate them to a pressing problem our family was then experiencing—a stack of unpaid bills for which we had no ready cash.

Six days after my vivid dream of the towels, my husband closed a lucrative deal. I found myself thinking, "Now we can *clean up* our debts, *wipe them out*," and this play upon words rang a memory bell that put me in mind of my dream.

Once I establish an association, it becomes a coding in my mind. Several times since this early dream, I have dreamed of stacks of washcloths and towels. The meaning is always the same—an increase in finances that clears debts.

The following is a later example of this process of building a logical associative code. One morning, during a stage when I was neither asleep nor yet awake, I had a vivid vision of a cigarette burning itself away. It did not occur to me to make an association with suicide because smoking was not then considered the desperate health hazard that it is today. However, some people, even at that time, were referring to cigarettes as "coffin nails." A few days later, the tragic meaning of the burning cigarette was revealed to me when the daughter of a friend committed suicide.

I was very bitter, for I had been able to save others from suicide who were only acquaintances. Why then did my friend have to lose her daughter? Why didn't the dream of the cigarette tell me more? I asked myself these questions over and over. Usually, I praise my dream faculty; but whenever the vision of the burning cigarette would come to mind, I would ask myself why at least the sex of the suicide the cigarette represented had not been revealed. That one clue might have led me to make a meaningful association with my friend's daughter in time to save her.

Six weeks ago, I had my second vision of a burning cigarette. This time the sex of the potential suicide was revealed plainly, for the cigarette was held in a pudgy male hand. As I emerged from the dream, I had a comforting intuitive thought, "Thank God it won't work." This intuition was correct. Before the end of the week, the son of a friend attempted suicide but was saved. In this instance, my sub-conscious had heeded the indirect scolding I had given it and had obliged me by revealing the sex of the suicide and by supplying me with more information than had been the case the first time I had been shown the symbol of the cigarette.

One good way to train and aid the subconscious toward ESP dreams is to build up a backlog of associative material. Bible reading provides a splendid frame of reference. At one time I was longing for the understanding and forgiveness of a friend. While this question was on my mind, I dreamed that I unwrapped a gift box and discovered a ring. All my dream books related rings to the marital hopes of single people. These meanings could not be applied to the life of a matron happily married for thirty-six years. I knew that I would have to find an associative meaning, so I started my mental processes: "Rings are round . . . gift . . . gift ring . . . ." In a flash, the associative processes of my mind solved the riddle by tuning me in to the unforgettable Biblical allegory of forgiveness—the story of the prodigal son whose father sym-bolized his understanding with the gift of a ring.

The public library also affords a gold mine of associative material. We can look up "The language of the flowers," and we can become familiar with state flowers and state flags. We should also know the birthstones for the different months of the year because they indicate time. There are also dic-tionaries of slang and encyclopedias of folklore.

In the previous chapter, I discussed dreams that are interpreted, mainly, through arbitrary coding to be found in popular dream books. Up to the present point in this chapter, I have discussed dreams that are interpreted solely by associa-tion. However, there are many complex dreams in which association must be blended with arbitrary coding. As our psychologists have pointed out, the dream condensation often allows one symbol to convey meanings on several levels of interpretation; this is true parapsychologically as well as psychologically.

The following example is a situation that led to a dream in which the main symbol had significance on both the associative and the coded levels.

At one time a wealthy friend of mine wanted my son, who was at that time just a teen-ager, and one of his buddies to cut down a tree on one of her properties. Even though my husband offered to supervise the job, I hesitated to give my consent, for tree cutting is a dangerous task that should be assigned to professionals. However, that night I had the following dream.

The Tree-Cutting Dream. I went to a window to hear a band that was playing outside. A crowd of people were gathering to see an entertainment of some kind that proved to be my husband and my son cutting down a large tree. At exactly the right moment, they abandoned the two-man saw they had been using and, grasping ropes, lowered the tree to the ground without mishap or crash. The crowd applauded as my husband and my son bowed like professional entertainers.

When I awakened from the dream, I knew I need have no fear concerning the tree-cutting adventure for which my son and his buddy and my husband were so avid. I'd have had still less fear had I known the true features this dream contained. Although my husband had expected a tree of only medium height, it was quite tall and full, like the tree in my dream. As my husband fastened ropes to the tree and told the two boys how to manipulate them, a group of neighbors gathered to watch. My husband then cut down the tree, which was gently lowered to the ground, without mishap or crash, by the two boys. The group of neighbors, which had grown to quite a crowd, burst into applause, and my husband and the two boys entertained them further with exaggerated stage bows.

Although the dream was obviously one that could be deciphered through association, I looked up the symbols in my dream book. Music was listed as an omen of success, a meaning I knew applied to the tree-cutting venture. Seeing a large tree cut down meant the death of a male relative. Applause meant an inheritance. It took several years for this coded prediction to come to pass, but the next death in my family was that of a male, and I did receive an inheritance.

Some objects are so strongly associative in the human mind that dream books would do well not to give them an arbitrary coding out of their own context. A washing machine is a good example of what I mean by a strongly associative symbol. Everything with which it is involved has to do with cleansing—water, soap, bleaches, etc. It is therefore unwise for dream books to code this machine with a meaning such as "an introduction to an important person" or "a trip to the country." However, in complex dreams featuring washing machines, coded symbols often blend in helpfully to provide a precognitive context.

One of my students was worried and unhappy about her pregnancy because of an Rh factor that made her obstetrician fear that she would have an unhealthy child. Then one night she had the following blessedly prophetic dream.

The Little Shirt in the Washing Machine Dream. The student was taking clothes out of her washing machine as her five-year-old son stood by watching. As she fished a tiny shirt from the suds, she thought she saw a stain down the front. But upon looking more closely at the shirt, she discovered that what had appeared to be a stain was a decorative emblem of an American flag. Then her five-year-old son piped up: "You don't have to worry at all about that little shirt, Mamma. It is going to come out OK."

My student knew at once that the dream meant that her baby's blood (represented by the red stripes of the flag) would be clean, free from the Rh taint. The coded meaning of the flag was also helpful, for in almost all dream books an American flag portends victory.

In the next example I shall recount, the coding in another washing machine dream helped a new student, who was not yet proficient in making associations, to achieve a correct interpretation. A group of children, four little boys and one little girl, were accused of a petty neighborhood vandalism, but all protested their innocence. That night my new student, who was the grandmother of the little girl, had the following dream.

The Clean Doll Dream. My student was at her washing machine doing the family wash. She reached down into the hot suds and, to her surprise and delight, lifted out a sparkling clean doll dressed in a ruffled silk gown that had not been damaged by the hot water.

My student's dream book told her that a doll represented a child in the life of the dreamer, and the student then understood her dream—her granddaughter, though "in hot water," was innocent. I agreed with my student. To me, the granddaughter was the "doll" among the four "guys"—an association with the slang expression "guys and dolls" in reference to men and women. Soon the little "guys" confessed that the little "doll" in the case was "clean."

As the above examples demonstrate, both the law of association and a system of arbitrary codes operate in our dreams. One of the reasons why the value of popular dream books was not discovered before the advent of my interpretive system is that these books present an arbitrary coding and then drop the matter without teaching that the principle of association is as necessary to dream divination as a code. The truth is that the law of association is necessary to most methods of divination, or applied parapsychology. In fact, these same two principal laws of divination, arbitrary coding combined with association, are also the main keys in my science of converting Rorschach-type ink blots to divinatory purposes. But in the final analysis, arbitrary coding is in itself an associative device. It is therefore safe to postulate that divination, from card reading to dreams, hinges upon one great law, the *law of association*.

5

How Realistically True Dreams Are Formed

Building on the principle of association as it must be used by our *conscious* thinking processes in order to interpret the ESP content of our dreams, we can now turn to a consideration of the role of the *subconscious* mind in utilizing association to build up paranormal dream messages. While previous chapters have emphasized dreams in which the ESP content has been hidden in symbols that must be deciphered by code or association, here we shall consider dreams that take a giant step into the future in a forthright manner, presenting fragments of precognition or entire productions that portray the future realistically, without dependence upon symbols.

Perhaps the first glimmering of ESP is to be found in occasional dreams in which the dream material, or a portion of it, appears to be associatively reversed. In these instances, instead of dreaming in association with an event of the past forty-eight hours, we dream of something we are to experience or see in the near future, usually a day or two after the dream occurs. The following is such an experience.

A recent acquaintance, who represented himself as an authority in his field, wanted my husband to join him in a venture in which the partnership would depend upon his knowledge and our capital. My husband did not doubt this man's ability, but he wanted to be sure he was of good character. That night I had the following dream.

The Bearded Dwarf Dream. I was looking down upon a male dwarf who possessed no body, consisting only of a large, ill-shaped head supported on legs barely six inches long. This head was aged and white-haired with a face terminating in a long, white beard that was dirty because it swept the floor.

Upon consulting the dream book I was using at the time, I was informed that dwarfs represent people who are not to be trusted. The dream told the same story associatively, for I had to look down upon this dream creature. And though the beard and the white hair indicated a knowledgeable person, the dirtiness of the beard revealed that the application of this knowledge would not be ethical.

Later in the day, an article about dwarfs came to my attention. Of the several dwarfs pictured, the expression on the face of one of them recalled my dream.

How can we account for the fact that the dwarf in this dream is a reversal of the usual order of association with the past forty-eight hours? How was the ESP determinant able to make an association with the picture I was to see the next day? I believe that in these instances the ESP determinant draws upon material stored in the preconscious prior to the past forty-eight hours. It may be that the dream faculty that is trained toward precognition reaches into the past for material more often than is the case when the dream faculty is untrained. The following dream is an illustration.

The Brown Wine Dream. I dreamed my husband was mixing a drink in the kitchen. Then he came into the family room where I was seated, handed me a wineglass filled with a bubbly, brown liquid, and said: "Here, taste this. How do you like it? Can you tell me what it is?" The liquid was sweet and delicious with a distinct wine flavor that was at once familiar and baffling. I could not guess the ingredients.

The next day a friend and her fourteen-year-old son came to visit me. As the woman and I talked, the boy amused himself with our pool table and television. Finally he announced, as though to impress us, that he was going to the liquor store to buy some wine. My friend and I paid no attention to the boy as he went out the door, for we knew he would not be allowed to purchase wine. However, when the boy returned, he went directly to the kitchen where I heard him open a bottle. Then he came into the living room and presented me with a paper cup that contained a brown, bubbly liquid. The taste was exactly that which I had experienced the night before—somewhat like wine, with a similarity to a delicious taste I could not identify. (Of course, the liquid was not wine. It was a soda pop made of raisins—the ingredient I could not identify in my dream.)

There was still another association with my dream of the night before—as he handed me the drink, the youth said: "Here, taste this. Do you like it? Can you tell me what it is?" The associative material that was used for the *Brown Wine Dream* was not of the past forty-eight hours. It harked back six months to the holidays when my husband had mixed a drink of his own concoction and, knowing that I do not have a taste for liquor, had presented his fancy drink with the words: "Here, drink this. Do you like it? Can you tell me what it is?" My memory of these words was reinforced by the fact that, for several days afterward, everytime I handed my husband a glass of water I would tease him by saying: "Here, drink this. Do you like it? Can you tell me what it is?"

There is a noticeable contrast between the ESP content of the *Bearded Dwarf Dream*, presented earlier in this chapter, and the *Brown Wine Dream*. The *Bearded Dwarf Dream* had a great deal of coded and associative value that enabled me to come to a decision regarding an important matter. The *Brown Wine Dream*, on the other hand, was simply a depiction of a most unimportant coming event. The coded meaning in my dream book did not apply nor was there any associative value that related to my affairs. The realistically true features of this dream stood only for the object (the wine) and the words I was to hear as it was presented to me the next day.

Not all realistically true dream fragments are dredged up from past months or years. Many contain remnants of the past forty-eight hours and, occasionally, both recent and more remote associations combine to present realistically true content. The following is such a dream.

The Dream of the Corpse Coming to Life. I dreamed that the funeral of a man who had passed away several years ago was still in progress. To my surprise and delight, the corpse lifted his hand and arm, opened his eyes, and sat up.

My first association was with an event that took place two days before this dream. A woman friend had told me of her visit to another woman friend who had been in the hospital in a state of coma for several days before passing away. The visitor was appalled that her friend had been shunted off into a lonely room outside of intensive care and that wet pads had been placed on her eyes. She removed the pads and entreated the sick woman to give her some sign of recognition. The woman responded by giving her a direct look and raising her hand and then her entire arm.

Turning to one of my dream books, I found that a corpse coming to life means the reception of a great honor. It is now four years since I had this dream, and no "great honor" has materialized. But the day after this dream, I saw a televised motion picture in which a corpse in a coffin raised first a hand and then an arm before coming back to life. If there was ESP value in my dream, it was a literal foreshadowing of the motion picture scene I have just described, and nothing else.

Some dreams that present an association with the coming

forty-eight hours can, of course, be ascribed to chance. However, when the dream faculty is trained, these dreams become so much more frequent than is the norm, and so finely detailed in their similarity to both the past and coming events with which they associate, that we know a good percentage of them have to be ESP productions.

Sometimes the ESP determinant makes an interesting conversion of associative material as a dream is in progress. Such dreams have been rare in my experience, but the following is one of them.

The Green Worms Dream. I dreamed that I was with my husband while he was taking a physical examination at a clinic. He tried to give a fecal specimen but instead passed two green worms. The nurse was not at all concerned and said the doctor need not examine the worms. I, however, was not at all sure of this, and I studied the worms apprehensively. They changed color before my eyes, turning from bright green to pale pink. Then they joined together, forming an intestine. I turned to the nurse. "The doctor must see this," I insisted. "It is something the doctor must take care of."

When I awoke and consulted my dream book, I was informed that a dream of worms warns against physical strain. A short time later, my husband informed me that he would have to go to the doctor and be fitted with a truss because he had developed a hernia. He then explained that he had the type of hernia in which an intestine drops and is in danger of protruding through a channel prepared for the passage of a testicle at birth.

At the mention of the word *intestine*, I found myself visualizing the intestine I had seen in my dream. It was a realistic presentation of the condition my husband and I were discussing. The dream was very meaningful, for the memory of the green worms keeps me alert to the fact that my husband must "avoid strain" by resting more and not lifting heavy objects.

Once again, there was an association with an event in the forty-eight hours prior to the dream. The day before this dream I had seen one of our cats pawing at a bright green worm in our garden. The ESP dream determinant (or determinants, as the case may be) had selected this association as a warning against strain, then had proceeded to elucidate by transforming the two worms into the flesh-colored intestine. I had been given a rare glimpse into the way in which a recent association stored in the preconscious can convert to a secondary past association to effect a paranormal presentation. No doubt the green worm tied in with a constellation of associations from which a choice could be made to structure ESP information. In this case we can relate the secondary association to the first almost without trying, for pictures of intestines look like worms. But not all transformed associations take place before our eyes as in this fortunate dream, for the dream faculty most often eliminates a showing of the first association and proceeds directly to the secondary when it wants to use it.

Some dreams are so paranormally constructed that they contain more than one realistic aspect of the future. In the following dream, an association with the previous day structured two realistic portrayals that were to occur the following day.

The Tax Accounting Dream. The day before this dream I stood on a busy street corner waiting for the light to change. A young evangelist—blissfully unaware that he was handing me a most interesting ESP experience, a machination of the devil, to him—pressed a tract into my hand. For the sake of being polite, I put the tract into my purse with the intention of destroying it when I reached home. But when I took the tract from my purse, I found it much more original than the usual "hell-fire and damnation" warnings, for the admonitions to "be saved" were pictorially portrayed.

The central character in these pictures was a hapless

individual whom I shall call "Mr. Nonbeliever." The first picture portrayed a grim-faced angel ruthlessly pulling Mr. Nonbeliever from his grave even as the poor man protested that it couldn't be possible because he was dead and therefore could know nothing about what was happening to him. In the next picture, Mr. Nonbeliever, still protesting the impossibility of the situation, stood before the throne of *the Almighty*. Scene after miserable scene of Mr. Nonbeliever's life was shown in retrospect as the *Voice of Judgment* intoned his transgressions in terms of *"He did do this,"* and *"He failed to do that."*

At that point, I closed the tract and destroyed it. Poor Mr. Nonbeliever was looking so thoroughly stupid and so hopelessly guilty that I did not want to witness the final scene in which I knew he would be told where he could go!

That night I dreamed I was going over my account books (an association with Mr. Nonbeliever's being called to "account" for his sins). I was very worried, and from time to time, I referred to a legal document accusing me of having done certain things I shouldn't have and of failing to do things I should have attended to. I felt extremely stupid and guilty as I read these accusations—an exact portrayal of Mr. Nonbeliever's final emotions. Finally, I picked up a pen and opened my checkbook (an association with Mr. Nonbeliever's being "checked" and his having to "pay the price" for his misdeeds). The dream came to a happy conclusion, for an unseen hand placed a packet of trading stamps—the kind that are issued with purchases and that can be *redeemed* in merchandise or cash (the psychological symbol for love)—on the checkbook before I had time to write out a check.

The very next day my mailbox contained some tax forms I had submitted to my tax consultant for his approval (the legal document of my dream). He also enclosed a letter telling me of certain mistakes I had made in my estimate and informing me that I had best come up with an additional $572.00 in order to prevent a fine. I felt extremely *stupid* and *guilty* as I read this letter, and I was chagrined to learn that I would have to part with much more money than I had estimated. My only consolation was that now I had an association for stamps. The meaning had eluded me before, but now it dawned on me that stamps have a direct relation to government matters. But why *trading stamps*? I was soon to find out.

I went to the telephone and called my husband, telling him that I had underestimated our taxes and that, in view of this mistake, I was sorry we had just purchased a new car. Then came a wonderful surprise. My husband informed me that more money than he had estimated had accrued to his commissions, and so we were well able to afford the new car. We were *redeemed* from penny pinching in order to meet the demands of the "infernal revenue," an expression many use to describe the Internal Revenue.

The predictive dream I have just recounted could not have been structured without the associations provided by the religious tract. These associations produced both predictive associative symbols and realistically true features of the coming day—the legal paper and my mood of guilt and stupidity.

While no one knows better than I that ESP is a multi-factored phenomenon—especially in cases of precognition—I am so convinced that the principle of association is a dominant determinant, even in ESP phenomena other than the dream, that I present the following theory for consideration. It may be that precognitive ESP occurs only on those occasions when an inner or an outer stimulus connects with preconscious material that relates to a coming event, either directly or through the successful activation of a secondary association. We must not forget that constellations of associative data are interlinked in the human mind and that an association can leap from constellation to constellation over the complex network of synapses.

When the mind is trained, or when the native ESP faculty is strong, this vital role in ESP experiences may not be so dependent upon chance as we might suppose. I have formulated a theory that the individual who has trained his mind toward the reception of ESP may at times be subconsciously guided toward associations that can be converted into paranormal preception. I describe this theory as CAI (*Compulsive Associative Input*), and I think it can best be illustrated by a further consideration of the *Green Worms Dream* presented earlier in this chapter. Was it just by chance that I decided to fill a few rare moments of idleness by taking a walk in the garden at the exact time my cat would call my attention to a worm that was to play a leading role in a meaningful dream message? Or did my subconscious prompt me to go outside instead of calling a friend on the telephone or picking up a book?

I can give a stronger example of CAI by turning the clock of history back to the year of 1968, the year of the assassination of Senator Robert Kennedy. I usually am not psychic unless engaged in card reading, blot making, or dreaming, but in May of that year I began to have some unpleasant experiences. As soon as I laid my head on my pillow, I seemed to tune in to a crowd of screaming, sobbing people. Also, I experienced the sensation of shaking internally, and I often felt uncomfortably tight in my solar plexus area.

I was not alone. Several of my friends who are psychic were experiencing similar symptoms. And one day when I purchased a book from a San Diego shop that specializes in ESP publications, the manager called me aside:

"Mrs. Sabin, are you picking up any indications of a national tragedy? Psychics who come in here are running scared. They don't know what they are afraid of but it is like sitting on a keg of dynamite. Are you getting anything that may explain these mass tensions?"

"No," I replied, "I am like the others. I know something of tragic moment is going to happen, but I don't know what it is."

Ironically, I had overlooked two card readings that did foretell the Senator's assassination. Shortly after the Senator had begun his campaign, I had programmed his name on a representative face card and slipped it into one of my reading decks. Twice, the Senator's card appeared with the message "an unfortunate occurrence" in regard to his campaign. But shortly after I received this message, one of the Senator's children became ill and had to be rushed to the hospital. I interpreted this event as the "unfortunate occurrence."

Months before, in November of 1967, I had received a message in the cards that was so nationally ominous that I called Western Union and had them send me a dated wire: "DEATH OF A HIGH U.S. OFFICIAL, A JUSTICE FIGURE." Then I proceeded to give the card symbols that predicted (1) the White House would be rocked and shocked by this death, and (2) the shock and fear it would bring to Vice-President Humphrey (whose representative face card was programmed into the deck at the time the prediction was made). As Attorney General of the United States, Senator Kennedy had once been the head of the Justice Department. And to hundreds of minority groups in this country, Robert Kennedy is regarded as one of the world's greatest champions of justice.

But by May of 1968, I had forgotten this prediction, which I had failed to associate with Robert Kennedy in the first place. Decoration Day came and went. Then, one day early in June, Senator Kennedy was campaigning in Oregon as I sat in a waiting room of a plush business office in Tijuana, Mexico. I had been in this waiting room many times before, and I had brought a good book along because waiting one's turn in Mexico is usually time consuming. But on that day, I had a strange compulsion to go to the window and look down upon a scene I knew would be dingy and depressing, for I was in the only modern building on the block. The pretty senorita at the desk frowned as I disturbed the soft interior lighting by rattling up a venetian blind, but I knew there was something I had to see. Looking across the street, my gaze fell upon a building over which was a large sign—*"Funeraria."* I do not speak Spanish, and my first association with this word was its first syllable, *fun*. It occurred to me, fleetingly, that I might be looking at a hobby shop or a shop specializing in joke items. Then I shuddered. Black curtains marked with the sign of the cross shrouded the windows. I knew I was looking at a funeral parlor. I was surprised by my own panic because I had once worked in the office of a funeral establishment. Deciding that I was unnerved because my first impression had been of fun, I went back to my seat.

Two hours later, I entered a business office across town from the first. The waiting room was crowded, so I settled down in the one available seat with my book—but not for long. Again I was standing at a window searching the street for something I felt I had to see. Then a sign over a window put me in mind of a hobby shop or a joke shop for just a fleeing instant before the full impact of its meaning hit my consciousness—*Funeraria!* I scuttled back to my seat, trying to forget the sight of the shrouded window with the sign of the cross. It was no use. My solar plexus area twisted into a knot. A faint nausea set in that was not to leave until I returned home for the night and went to bed—only to dream.

The Dream of the Two Bells. I was in the cemetery decorating the graves of family members and friends. After I placed the last flower, I looked toward the summit of a hill expecting to see a monument that is a distinguishing feature of the cemetery, three gigantic bells hanging within a graceful arrangement of arches. But there were only two bells and two arches! Why?

I woke up, still wondering. I told myself that the dream was an association with my recent visit to the cemetery on Decoration Day and went back to sleep—again to dream.

The Fluttering Moth Dream. This time I was back in a house in which I had given many parties. I glimpsed company through the window, so I opened the front door to let in a group of people most of whom were young. How jubilant they were! How gay! They had come for a celebration of some kind, and some already wore party hats. It did not seem at all odd in the dream that two blackbirds entered the room with the guests, flying right over their heads, and I paid them little attention. Then a voice said: "Look at those two blackbirds. Look at what they are doing." The dream scene changed. I was looking at a large, brown moth fluttering over a garden pond. The two blackbirds swooped down, one right after the other, and the cruel beak of the first bird clamped down upon the moth that fluttered helplessly in the last throes of death.

I woke up, switched on my light and reached for my note pad. "Dear God!" I wrote. "Two Funerarias! Two bells! Two blackbirds! What do these death signs mean? Two deaths or a death within a two?" I got up, made myself a pot of coffee, and ran the cards. All family members perfectly safe. I relaxed and went back to bed. I am an optimist by nature, and the next day I was able to busy myself with a research project. Later in the day I went to my room and could not believe my eyes. The large brown moth of my dream was fluttering about. I reflected briefly on the short lifespan of moths. This poor creature had little time left. Opening the door to the garden, I watched the moth flutter out. "Be happy while you can," I thought.

June sixth was bright and beautiful. Beglamoured by the whirlwind campaign of Robert Kennedy, California Democrats went to the polls to vote him in. Late that night I went to the television and tuned in to the Senator's headquarters. A huge, jubilant crowd had assembled, and I noticed that many of them were young people. A few wore campaign hats—the "party" hats of my recent dream, but I failed to make the association at the time. The Senator spoke briefly and charmingly in perhaps one of the most triumphant and joyful moments of his life, then he left the platform. I left the television on but went back to my research project, which had reached a most interesting point. Then I jumped from my chair. Had I heard aright? It sounded as though an announcer had stated that there was a rumor that the Senator had been shot. My son, who had been engrossed in a book at the other end of the room, made a dash for the television, turning up the volume as our attention galvanized on tragedy. Laughter was turning to screams and tears. Someone was pleading: "Is there a doctor in the house? Is there a doctor in the house?" Then the terrible scenes of the strife in the kitchen of the Ambassador Hotel, the cameras coming in for a closeup of the fallen Senator. One eye stared glassily ahead while the eyelid of the other fluttered helplessly, reminding me of the horror of my dream. The fluttering moth was caught in the grim beak of death!

I staggered to a chair. Now I knew the portent of the two funerarias, the two bells, and the two blackbirds—a second Kennedy assassination!

Before closing this account, I want to point out an association between the two Mexican funeral parlors, the jubilant crowd in the *Fluttering Moth Dream*, and the people celebrating the Senator's election. As you recall, I first associated the word funeraria with the word fun, and in both my dream and the final scenes of the Senator's life, fun and frolic preceded death! Perhaps this is a case of CAI. My subconscious may have compelled me to seek out the funeral parlors in order to gather impressions necessary to build up dreams portending a national tragedy.

And we are still faced with the problem of the real moth that I discovered the day after the *Fluttering Moth Dream*. Remember, I pitied this creature because I knew it did not have long to live!

The moth is only one of many objects that have appeared in my life after having been foreshadowed in a dream the night before. As I write this paragraph, I can shift my gaze to a vase that was dreamed in all its details the night before I received it as a gift. The material of the vase is the same as in the dream—glass. It is the same height as my dream vase and the same shape. It is fluted as in the dream and has the same scalloped rim. There is a very slight difference in the color shade, the one in the dream being a bit more amber and the real vase being a bit more green, though it looks entirely amber in the sunlight, where it was placed when I first saw it.

But there is a difference between the dreams of the moth and the vase. The moth was in itself symbolic. The vase was not. Nor can I attach a dream meaning, either coded or symbolic, that has come to pass. The dream falls into the category of a realistically true presentation of a coming situation.

I have never experienced a long dream that was realistically true, and I rarely have short dreams of this nature. More frequently, I have a few realistically true fragments in a dream that is otherwise symbolic of a code or slanted toward associative interpretation. However, a few long, detailed, realistically true dreams have been reported by reputable people, but these occur only once or twice in a lifetime—perhaps because there are seldom enough pertinent associations in the preconscious that can lead back to the many necessary past associations in the exact order necessary to structure such dreams. Also, such dreams are often reinforced by telepathic factors.

But complex though the role of association is, in structuring our dreams, forthcoming chapters will teach you how to harness this principle to your great advantage.

6

Id Dreams That Lack ESP

In previous chapters I have propounded the theory that a psychological wish fulfillment purpose, either latent or simple, can lead us into a dream area our psychologists have not yet explored—that wondrous domain, incredible even in the strange land of our dreams, where we can find the answers to our questions and catch glimpses of future events. However, I must now qualify this theory by mapping out dangerous dream terrain of which you must beware—quicksands of either certain *depth psychology wish fulfillment* presentations or *anxiety wish situations* in which ESP flounders helplessly, losing all control of the wish element (which proceeds along lines of least resistance to fulfill itself in accord with a desire that may or may not be compatible with truth).

In order to understand these pitfalls, we must gain an insight into frontiers of dream wish fulfillment theory into which our psychologists have already ventured, breaking the way and establishing paths of knowledge with which we should become familiar. I am referring to two specific dream categories that will be explained in the next three chapters:

1. *Id dreams*: Dreams in which the wish fulfillment originates in the unconscious. The wish is a repressed desire of a forbidden nature and is therefore not forthright and recognizable, but *latent* or hidden (discussed in Chapters 6 and 7).

2. *Ego dreams*: Dreams in which the wish fulfillment originates in the *subconscious* or preconscious (the memory bank from which ideas and impressions can be recalled). Because the wish fulfillment is forthright and easily recognized, it is called *simple* (discussed in Chapter 8).

When the desires of id dreams surface in forms so common to the race that our psychologists consider them classical examples, they are often devoid of ESP, especially if they are emotionally impacted. Later in this chapter I shall present examples of these dreams, but first I must discuss their background.

We do not always understand nature or those insane wishes that sometimes loom up from the depth of the unconscious or id to haunt the minds of the most rational during dreams, or sometimes even for a few seconds during waking hours. Sigmund Freud discovered that our dreams usually express wishes that have been repressed and that these wishes often appear in our dreams carefully disguised in a *manifest* content that keeps us from realizing their secret or *latent* wish fulfillment. Because our culture demands the repression of many of our sex desires, this subject is usually the theme of the latent or disguised dream content. This discovery was most important to therapeutic psychiatry, for the study of a neurotic's or a psychotic's dreams leads to a diagnosis and sometimes to the healing of mental ailments.

Most mental illnesses that are not situational grow from

two roots implanted in the unconscious: (1) atavistic memories of sadistic or sexual practices that were once common to man but that, like cannibalism and incest, have been given up in the interests of society; (2) stages of infant sexual life that have been outgrown, forgotten, and repressed.

At night we all go crazy, to a certain extent, because that part of the *self* or *ego* that enables our conscious thinking processes to function during the day is asleep, and the moral guard is down. The unconscious or *id* can then take advantage of the situation to surface old desires, which it has never forgotten, into wish fulfillment dreams that are usually so camouflaged that they can't be recognized when we wake up. In these instances, we cannot hope to make a psychological interpretation until we apply the two keys given above—regression to atavistic tendencies or to outgrown stages of infant sexual life. Furthermore, we can't afford to forget that atavistic and outgrown tendencies are interrelated.

To the sexually squeamish, Freud's theory that infants experience a degree of sexual life is revolting—a neurotic's debasement of the innocence of little children. But when speaking of "infant sexuality," Freud did not intend the full connotation of the terminology that the evil-minded read into it. The truth is that during the first five years of the infant's life nature is very busy, ushering the child through a bio-psychological program designed to prepare him for the successful performance of the adult sex role that he is later to fulfill if the race is to survive. If you are not yet acquainted with Freud's infant psychology, you soon will be, for I must give a brief outline in order for you to know how to evaluate the ESP content of your dreams. I shall be killing two birds with one stone, for you will learn that the sexual patterns found in children are normally so mild, at least on the conscious level, that nature is able to accomplish her purpose while leaving the conscious innocence of children basically intact.

Psychologically, the time during which an infant sucks at the mother's breast, or a facsimile of the breast, is denoted as the *oral stage*. During this phase, the sexual implications are merely an awakening of the *libido*, or pleasure principle, that will be the dominant inducement in the future sex relationship for which the child is being prepared. Severe disturbances during this oral stage can cause neurosis later in life. Some dreams of drinking hark back to the oral stage, and if such dreams are recurrent, we can judge that they are too emotionally rooted to have ESP value. However, the occasional dreams of drinking or experiencing "a slip 'twixt the cup and the lip" are predictive, at least for the dream-trained mind, as Chapter 11 will illustrate.

A second phase experienced by the infant is called the *anal sadistic stage*, which is provided by nature to teach many lessons. The pleasure principle is experienced as the child learns to exert a conscious control over the retention or expulsion of feces. He is exerting his will and performing his first "work." He learns to become determined and purposeful and tries to rule his environment by being destructive and aggressive. When this stage is accomplished successfully, it helps individuals to become goal oriented with the fortitude it takes to win life's battles. But a fixation in, or a regression to, the anal sadistic stage can produce sex perversion in which release can be found only in inflicting cruelty upon another. If such a tendency is not overt, but merely latent, it often influences dreams.

Abnormal psychology is almost always ugly, and in one psychiatrist's report, a woman often dreamed that she was beating her little daughter with a horse whip. She loved the little girl dearly in waking life, but in the dream she thrilled from the top of her head to the tips of her toes as the cruel whiplashes drew blood. There is no ESP in this dream but only an indication of an emotional disturbance with both homosexual and anal sadistic tendencies raging just beneath the surface of consciousness. All recurring dreams of cruelty to others, or dreams in which the infliction of cruelty brings the dreamer pleasure, are, in general, devoid of ESP.

Many people prefer not to admit that infants normally go through an early phase of discovering and exploring their genitals. Freud called the practices of this stage *autoeroticism* or self-love, and because he was a sensitive man, he was shocked when he learned that some people had the idea that he implied a full sexual expression. During the autoerotic stage, nature is again performing an important task, endeavoring to help the child achieve a proper identification with his own sex. Needless to say, if nature accomplishes her purpose, a safeguard has been set up against homosexuality in later life.

During the autoerotic stage, the mores of civilization and the heavy, body-enveloping nightclothes into which we bundle our children result in repression. More than this, some parents find the self-exploration of children so revolting that, unwisely, they inflict punishment. Freud expressed the theory that the reason neurosis is uncommon among savages may be because their children are allowed free sexual expression. However, he could not endorse this freedom for upper stratas of civilization, for he thought it detrimental to cultural achievements. Suppression through diversion is most likely the right approach to correction. Certainly there is no cause for shame on the part of the parent, for autoeroticism is usually always an occurrence during the early years of the gifted child.

When a child attains the age of five or six, nature usually abandons her program of identification through autoeroticism, and the genitals are forgotten in a *latent stage* that lasts until puberty. The desire at this time is for a love object other than the self, and the young adult works toward dating and marriage.

I shall deal with autoerotic dreams in the next chapter for they often relate to ESP content.

The overlapping oral, anal sadistic, and autoerotic stages are complicated by still another nature-ordained process of biopsychological development. It is too bad that Freud did not coin words to replace "parental incest" when teaching his discovery of the *Electra stage* in which girl infants are attracted to their fathers and the corresponding *Oedipus stage* during which male infants form an attachment to the mother that has romantic overtones. Incest is a brutal term for the mild degree of conscious desire and fulfillment that a physically and emotionally undeveloped child can experience, but the term is psychologically correct, for it relates to atavistic tendencies to actual incest that the race has only recently outgrown.

However, the infant does not experience the Oedipus-Electra stage because the race of man is sinful and perverse. Again, nature is about the business of preparing the child for the adult role that is to come. Both the unconscious incestuous desires and the more mild conscious attraction to the parent of the opposite sex create a normal sex pattern that will be followed after puberty. Therefore, it goes without saying that cases of homosexuality can result from disturbances during the Electra or Oedipus stages. If some event or series of events causes a fixation upon the parent of the opposite sex, loyalty to this parent may make a heterosexual relationship impossible. The sudden removal of a parent during the Electra or Oedipus stages is very dangerous, for the child needs a parent of his own sex with whom to make a sexual identification as well as a parent of the opposite sex for heterosexual attraction.

Even those of us who are the best adjusted regress, at times, to outgrown Electra or Oedipus desires in our nocturnal productions. A dream in which we deeply mourn the death of the parent of the same sex as ourselves is seldom predictive of such an event. Usually it is a regression to infantile wishes that the parent of the same sex, who is our rival, "go away" (the infant's concept of death) and leave us a clear field for the affections of the parent of the opposite sex. Such desires are seldom remembered, for nature concludes the Electra or Oedipus stage early in childhood. Even when this phase is in full progress, other interests of infant life, during which so much must be learned, distract the child's attention from the experience.

Dreams of the death of one's mate or betrothed usually relate back to the Electra or Oedipus stage in an indirect way. A young woman in my neighborhood had a recurring dream that her fiancé, whom she loved ardently on the conscious level, was killed in a car accident. She would wake up crying, sure that her sweetheart was fated for death before they could be married. But her wedding day came and went. Eight weeks after this joyous event, the bride had a nervous breakdown and went into therapy. A deep, subconscious father fixation was discovered and treated until this young woman was able to resume her marital life. The dream was not predictive. The wish fulfillment was so strongly oriented psychologically that it made no deviation toward ESP. Subconsciously, the dreamer had wished to remain with her father, and her recurring dream fulfilled this wish.

Dreams of the deaths of brothers or sisters during which we feel deep distress are also often vestiges of the Electra or Oedipus stage, for our siblings are rivals for parental affections. Sometimes dreams camouflage brothers or sisters as small animals. When an elderly man of my acquaintance found that he was facing death within a few months, he felt he wanted to go back East to see two younger brothers who still lived on the family farm. However, whenever he dreamed he was back in the farmhouse he wished to visit, his brothers did not appear. Instead, he found himself killing two rats who were trying to attack him. The dream was so upsetting that he decided not to take the trip.

On the conscious level, no nine-year-old girl ever wished for a little sister more than I, possibly because the younger sister of a playmate my own age was very dear to me. However, there was a conflict between my conscious desire and my sub-conscious hate and fear, as the following dream will reveal.

The Strange, Small Animal Dream. I dreamed I walked into our dining room and saw a large bird cage hanging in the corner. As I drew closer to the cage, I saw that it contained a small animal, hardly bigger than a large rat, yet more grotesque and fierce than anything else on the face of the earth. Then, to my horror, the strange little animal forced the door of the cage open and leaped at me. I awoke screaming.

In the Freudian sex symbology, a cage can stand for a womb; a Freudian play upon words would convert "strange little animal" into "a little stranger," a term often used to describe a newly-born child.

Recently, at a party, a woman asked me to interpret the following dream.

The Mirror Dream. "I walked into my bedroom and was shocked to see my deceased husband waiting for me. I ignored him and went over to my mirror, for the thought occurred to me that he had come to take me with him in death. When I looked into my mirror, I was happy to see that I was fat and ugly. 'My husband can't want me.' I thought, 'he has come for my sister who is much younger and still pretty.' "

After recounting this dream, the woman who confided it added hopefully: "I think this dream means that my sister is going to die. We have never been close. She is very strange and unfeeling with an ugly disposition."

I left this woman with her own interpretation, for one can't explain depth psychology at parties, nor can one reveal that an ugly mirror image seen in a dream often reflects faults of our own that we refuse to see by projecting them upon others. We must forgive the dreamer, however, for she is the victim of a father fixation. Her dream harks back to subconscious wishes at the time of her courtship that it is the younger sister, not she, who will be taken in marriage and leave the father.

If there is any precognition in this dream, I doubt that it portends the death of the sister, for this is both the conscious and the unconscious wish of the dreamer.

A further complication of Electra or Oedipus death dreams is the fact that death wishes are often masked by a displacement of persons. Over twenty years ago, a male student dreamed that he was weeping bitterly at the bier of President Truman, who was then still alive. The dream was purely psychological, with President Truman substituted for the dreamer's father who was also alive at that time. The psychological giveaway is, as usual, the deep grief of the dreamer who felt no great affection for Truman in waking life.

But devoid of predictive ESP though the types of dreams presented in this chapter are, they contain the possibility of *prognostication*, especially if they are recurrent. It is highly unlikely that a mother who dreams repeatedly of beating her little girl for pleasure can remain a good mother throughout the years. In the case of the dreamer who kept dreaming her fiancé would perish in a car accident, was there not great danger that his life would be wrecked by his wife's mental illness? And perhaps it was just as well that the elderly man who kept dreaming of killing rats in his old home did not go to visit his brothers. Not that he would have attacked them physically, but with a subconscious animosity and fear so great as his, he might have spoiled the visit with slights and accusations of projected faults.

Paradoxically, it is always the true dream that makes parapsychological dream interpretation difficult. In Chapter 3, I explained that on rare occasions a realistically true dream, such as Lincoln's dream of his own death defeats the accuracy of deciphering by code. In Chapter 5, I explained that occasionally the realistically true dream reverses the order of an associative presentation. Now I must warn my readers that occasionally emotionally impacted dreams of danger for a loved one or for ourselves may not be a production of the id but a true depiction. Whether or not precognitive dreams of accidents or deaths are emotional, they are a blessing in those instances in which action can be taken to prevent the tragedy. Proof that such dreams are precognitive lies in the fact that though the danger has been avoided, other elements of the dream remain exactly as they were foreseen.

7

The ESP Role
of the Censor

In this chapter, we shall make a particular observation of dreams in which the ESP determinant, or determinants, utilize a component of the dream called the *censor* to forward ESP content. By this time, even those readers who are not well informed in psychology have a fairly good idea that the censor acts in two ways: (1) to mask and camouflage a repressed wish of a sexual nature so that the conscience will not be offended when the dream is recalled; (2) to combine, sometimes, with masochistic tendencies to punish even a camouflaged dream.

For instance, in Chapter 2 I recounted *The Thanksgiving Dream* in which a man dreamed he was once again a youth celebrating this feast with his parents, the odd part of the dream being that he was seated at a table with his mother while his father sat at another table with his two brothers. Because a table represents the sex act in the Freudian set symbols, the dream is clearly an Oedipus production in which an old wish for the exclusive affection of the mother is granted. The utterance of the father, "Hand me the bird," is a bit punitive, indicating that the father has a first claim on the mother. However, this remark affords an associative play upon words, for it suggests a proverb, "A bird in the hand is worth two in the bush," that answered the dreamer's question as to whether he should take an offer for his property or wait for a better deal.

Because this and the previous chapter deal with dreams having their origins in outgrown autoerotic or Oedipus-Electra desires, I wish to digress from the subject of ESP long enough to state that people who have occasional dreams that are strongly marked psychologically are neither wicked nor fated for insanity. Repetitive dreams may be indicative of a neurosis, but Freud discovered that in the main, healthy people have many of the same dreams that are experienced by the mentally ill. Actually, the dreamer of autoerotic or Oedipus dreams is often a person of strong character who has been successful in suppressing wishes and desires that he considers unworthy or inappropriate. Furthermore, dreams of this type can indicate a strong native psyche with libido energy that can be channeled into the arts and sciences. The genius is often a person in whom regressive tendencies are not strong enough to create a crippling neurosis or a psychosis, but only strong enough to affect his dreams or a small area of his conscious life.

My own dreams can be seen to contain Freudian symbols, but these same symbols operate on other levels as well. As Freud has demonstrated, our dreams are strongly compacted, exhibiting a *condensation* in which one symbol can embody several meanings. In the first chapter of this book, I recounted my *Cruel Ghost Dream*, which contains two repressions, autoeroticism and the Electra complex. When Freud examined the dreams of his own children he discovered only wishes that he considered *simple*, such as eating candy bars. However, since food stands for love and libido situations, these dreams may have been more psychologically impacted than they first appear. Many of my own childhood dreams, like the *Cruel Ghost Dream*, were sophisticated on Freudian levels of which I was entirely innocent in the waking state. But as Freud has said, the unconscious of the child is closely connected with the unconscious processes of its parents.

As you may recall, the *Cruel Ghost Dream* begins with the fulfillment of a simple wish, one of my forbidden but indulged in pleasures, a ride for a few blocks on a streetcar. I am joined by a ghostly figure (an impression gained from a parent in nightclothes, according to Freud) who strikes terror to my heart. This terror is justified when the ghost punctures my throat with a chisel (a tool my father often used and also a Freudian symbol of the penis). The repression of Electra tendencies is obvious. The dream also relates to autoeroticism because my mother had often told me that masturbation would result in a *puncture* that would render me unable to hold my urine. I would thereafter have to sit on the toilet day and night and could never go out to play. Clever manipulation by the censor displaced the erotic zone and replaced pleasure with pain in a move that also allowed precognition, for I was soon to swallow a piece of metal that punctured my throat.

Now, what is the mechanism of the censor who so cleverly disguised the sex implications of this dream while at the same time either independently making these implications precognitive or working under the direction of ESP determinants toward this end?

Between the unconscious (id) and conscious (ego) levels of the mind there is the subconscious or preconscious. The preconscious contains a storage mechanism for information that we do not use every day but that we can usually recall at will. There is much evidence that the preconscious is more than a memory bank, for it has its own known drives and activities as is the case with the unconscious. One entity or structure of the preconscious is the superego, an associative system that forms the basis for the conscience, that "still small voice" that keeps us aware of what is right and what is wrong. Originally, this superego structure was formed from the teachings and admonitions of the parents. Later the structure is expanded by the mores of society and our own thinking processes. The superego is parental in that it is protective, keeping us from pleasures that are, in the long run, harmful to ourselves and to the race. At night, when the ego is at rest, the superego is still on guard. It allows the unconscious, or id, to release the tensions of repression, but only to a certain degree, for it masks and camouflages these desires, perhaps so that they will not be able to influence us down the primrose path the next day. When the superego uses techniques such as symbols, substitute people, displacements, etc., to alter the dream, it is called the *censor*.

And since this censor is so crucial to the ESP content, I shall devote the rest of this chapter to its operations in id dreams relating to autoerotic or Electra-Oedipus wish fulfillment.

Autoerotic Dreams Having ESP Content

Emotionally impacted autoerotic dreams are often delightful, gravity-defying experiences of effortless gliding, dancing, or flying. In these dreams the censor displaces pleasure from the genital area and allows it to express itself in an ecstasy of general élan. These dreams, though generally devoid of precognition, are related to another area of interest to parapsychology—out-of-the-body experiences known as "astral travel" in occult circles. Sometimes sleepers become conscious of two bodies—the inert form on the bed and a far more interesting counterpart that is free of physical grossness yet alive with the consciousness of the projected individual. Although many of these experiences of the exteriorization of a second body are preceded by dreams of flying, the projections are not limited to this type of dream.

Those flying dreams that do not pull attention to the experience of ecstasy are the best suited either for exteriorization or for an adaption toward ESP content. Dreams of dancing or gliding that are not thrillingly pleasurable can be coded to mean accomplishment of a project with ease or grace. If we have a partner, a project in which we are or shall be working with another will be realized easily and pleasantly. To see loved ones or friends dancing has the same connotations for them. To see strangers dancing means an easier and more pleasant period of life for the dreamer.

Another common theme in autoerotic dreams, one in which the censor is more amenable to precognitive content, is the playing of a musical instrument. Flying and dancing dreams are necessarily limited as to coded possibilities, whereas the playing of a musical instrument offers the ESP dream determinants a wide selection of objects from which to choose when structuring a message. Thus we can code that playing a violin means a romantic love interest, whereas playing the piano can stand for the meaning given in our popular dream book references.

A few years ago, I dreamed that I was once again a teen-ager. Seated at a grand piano, I was playing Chopin's difficult but rewarding "Crystal Ballroom" while my first beau hovered over me with ardent but most respectful attention. I stopped playing and made a little speech of self-appreciation. "I am very happy," I told my beau, "that I am able to extract every nuance of expression from my music. You will note that I observe every pause, every crescendo, and every diminuendo. Nothing is left out. I play this music exactly as it is written."

At the time this dream occurred, I had sold the pocket book rights of my *Cybernetic ESP Breakthrough* to Award Books, and I was apprehensive that they might make alterations and deletions. These fears were put to rest when I opened my dream book and was informed that playing the piano means the publication of a written effort. I knew then that the dream had more than the psychological implications of autoeroticism being diverted to a love object. The coding and my spoken words in the dream were correct. My book was published exactly as I had written it.

Oedipus-Electra Dreams Having ESP Content

Fortunately, not all Oedipus-Electra dreams are stereo-typed depictions of the death of the parent of the opposite sex, or the death of a sibling or of a fiancée or mate, as was the case with dreams discussed in the last chapter. Sometimes the repressed Electra or Oedipus longings surface in episodes in which the censor allows a more direct, yet still masked, expression of sex interest but makes a substitution of persons that can be difficult to detect, as was the case in the following dream.

The Atomic Flash Dream. I dreamed that my husband and I were both sleeping, but in the dead of the night I woke up. To my surprise, I saw a person enter our bedroom, a young man of our acquaintance who is a top security chemist with access to secrets of the United States government. As the young man came toward me, the outside world and my room lit up with a blinding flash that consumed him and burned me with a physical suffering that was almost unbearable. In the dream, I thought that the young man had revealed United States' secrets to an enemy nation who had bombed us. My suffering was compounded by the fact that the entire city had been stricken and that both my husband and my son had been burned as badly as I.

The next night, a thunderstorm came up, and a blinding flash knocked out all the electrical facilities in our area of San Diego. As our house lit up and rocked with a jolting crash, my son, who was standing before a metal heater, grabbed his leg and yelled. The next second, he was laughing as he explained that he had experienced a mild electrical shock.

In this instance, the censor both aided and impeded ESP content. Flashes of lightning symbolize the sex act, and we must give atomic flashes the same connotation.

There may be a few exceptions to the rule that deeply emotional dreams have little to do with ESP, and at first consideration, the *Atomic Flash Dream* seems to be one of these. It was filled with both physical and mental suffering—definitely more than just a bad dream, for it was a full-fledged nightmare.

The astute and intuitive Freud was of the opinion that the censoring superego is not fully responsible for dreams that are terribly punitive. He reasoned that perhaps some masochistic tendency in the dreamer's psychology somehow gains the upper hand in these awful dream situations. Today we know that the individual's physiological chemistry has a great deal to do with his mental health and with his dreams. In Chapter 11 I shall have more to say concerning the effect of inner stimuli upon dreamers, but let us now return to an analysis of the wish fulfillment element and the work of the censor in the *Atomic Flash Dream*.

The camouflaged desire for sex with someone other than my husband was at no time in the manifest material of this dream. The censor stepped in before I could develop an emotional or physical response to the image of the young chemist. I wasn't afraid of him, either, just wondering what he was doing in my bedroom at that hour of the night. The wish fulfillment is not the death wish that so often occurs in Electra-Oedipus type dreams at the expense of ESP content. No one dies though the city is annihilated and my loved ones and I are badly injured.

Furthermore, nothing in this dream was a response to a recent desire in my waking consciousness. I had no penchant whatever for the young man in my dream. He simply did not appeal to me, either in physical or personality traits, though I did admire his fine mind whenever I could get him on the track of science, which was seldom, for he was really coming to my Applied ESP Research Society for a diversion from science instead of the dedicated activity I had expected.

I decided to do a little dream sleuthing to find out the real identity of the man in my dream, so I began by writing down the names and general descriptions of the men in my life. I did not have far to go. The young chemist of whom I had dreamed had the physical build and the mannerisms of my deceased father-in-law! Here was the "father figure" substituted by the censor in place of my own father. "The next time the censor wishes to fool me about an incestuous wish fulfillment," I thought, "it will have to use a composite, or bring in a king or one of the United States presidents." Even as these thoughts ran through my mind, I remembered how the clever censor had used still another father substitute years before—but before recounting this dream I must reveal the circumstances that led up to it.

Shortly after my mother passed away, my stepfather, who had come into my life when I was twenty, revealed that he had made out his will entirely in favor of one heir, whose identity he would not disclose. I thought the heir must be one of his blood relatives or one of my cousins whose company he preferred to mine. Naturally, I wished that I would be the one to inherit the estate my mother had helped build up, but I said nothing. Shortly after being told about the will I had the following dream.

The Wedding Preparation Dream. I was in the ladies' dressing room of a church preparing for my wedding as the guests assembled. As I applied lipstick, the image in the mirror informed me that I was young and attractive. Finally, I donned my bridal veil, which was a white stole I still owned in waking life that had been given to me on the occasion of my daughter's wedding two years before. Suddenly a compulsive curiosity tempted me. I knew it was a breach of etiquette to show myself before the wedding; nevertheless, I walked out to the center of the church platform and surveyed the guests. Then I knew I was searching for a particular person, though I did not know whom. Suddenly the room grew dark, but by peering intently I was able to see the face of the person whom I sought. It was my stepfather.

When I consulted my dream book the next day, I was informed that preparing for a wedding meant an inheritance. The dream was true. At the time of my stepfather's death, I was his sole heir. The first wish fulfillment is to be young and attractive again. The second wish is atavistic to childhood. I "take the center of the stage" by exhibiting myself, though I know it is a "breach of etiquette." This verges on the child's wish to be seen in the nude by its elders, especially elders of the opposite sex. And there is still another latent factor, one that harks back to the tendency of a child to peer through the darkness in the hope of an intimate glimpse of the parent of the opposite sex. The censor makes the dream acceptable by substituting a father figure, the stepfather who did not come into my life until I was twenty, for my actual parent. And it is this same stroke of creative genius that brings the dream to a logical conclusion, for my stepfather is necessary to the paranormal content. Oddly enough, the darkness that set in and obscured my vision of the people in the church was a help instead of a hindrance, for it shrouded all the people except my stepfather, thus aiding me to find him.

Here is another Electra-tinged dream that contains ESP content. It was reported to me by a student who had trained her dream faculty with my techniques.

The Fatherly President Dream. The student, a woman of middle age, dreamed that she was sitting in a railroad station with President Nixon. As though she were a small child, she placed her head on his lap as the dream faded out.

I told this student that the wish fulfillment was compounded of both an atavistic desire for parental protection and security and overtones harking back to the Electra complex—one of my clues to the latent content being the censor's making sure that the dream faded out as soon as contact with the fatherly image was accomplished.

On the ESP level, my student knew that railroad stations denote change in the symbolic sense and travel in the literal sense. Both situations were soon to apply to Mr. Nixon. Snapping out of the lethargy of his first years in office, he brought about many surprising changes, including a diplomatic trip to Red China. Although these changes were bewildering to my right-wing student, she was unafraid, for she knew her dream had told her she could "rest assured" that the protective overtones of the dream indicated the wisdom and the safety of the changes the president was accomplishing.

To me, the most interesting feature of this dream is that the student's dream censor had used the same method that my censor had employed in the *Wedding Preparation Dream* to forward ESP content through the substitution of a father figure in an Electra situation.

The crucial role of latent dream material and the censor's handling of this material to forward ESP content flies in the face of professional opinion. Dr. Carl Jung revealed that in the paranormal dreams that were brought to his attention, the ESP content was always in the manifest, never the latent, material as is the case with dreams presented in this chapter. But we must remember that our psychologists and parapsychologists have had a limited number of ESP dreams presented to them. Because the majority of the people have not been trained to appraise the paranormal value of their dreams, only the more obvious examples have been reported. We must remember, also, that there is a psychological disagreement as to what does, or does not, constitute latent material. To Jung and his disciples, who negate the Electra-Oedipus complexes and hidden wish fulfillment of a sexual nature, latency is admitted only in those dreams in which the dreamer himself discovers a sexual significance in a dream symbol. With this degree of limitation, it is little wonder that Jungian psychologists have been unable to find ESP in latent material. A final handicap in the recognition of ESP dream content by our psychological professionals lies in the fact that they have not, to date, studied the productions of those who have trained the dream faculty to use association and an arbitrary code to forward ESP content.

But even with my more complete view of dream functioning, I am unable to pinpoint the ESP determinant in any one area of the dream. Certainly the preconscious with its provision of stored associative material and its exercise of censorship is a heavy contributor. But in the next chapter, when we progress from id to ego dreams, I shall reveal that the preconscious can impede, as well as forward, paranormal dream material.

8

How to Interpret
Ego Dreams

Because I am the first person to make a total exploration of the dream, I am posting a sign of danger as I break parapsychological paths for others to follow. This sign, which is always suspect in the paranormal evaluation of dreams, spells out *emotion!*

In Chapters 6 and 7, I explained that certain classifications of emotionally impacted id dreams are too purely psychological to have paranormal significance; while on the other hand, there are id dreams in which the underlying psychology of the latent wish fulfillment can forward predictive material. This chapter will follow the same format, but with dreams that are not of the id but of the ego. You will be taught how to discount emotionally impacted dreams of simple wish fulfillment and how to recognize ego dreams in which the simple wish can sometimes forward an ESP content.

The habit of our dreams to grant our wishes is the main reason psychologists and psychiatrists consider dreams incapable of casting future events in a true light, except by chance. The ego dream, especially, will often either magnify a current anxiety or fulfill a current wish. Unlike the id dream, the wish fulfillment of the ego dream is not an emotional aborigine stealing up from the jungle of repressed or outgrown desires. The ego dream is born in the area of the preconscious, which is located between the conscious and unconscious territories of the human mind. Memories in this mental territory can usually be recalled at will. Here reside new and dangerous memory inhabitants that are hostile to the ESP content: (1) residues of current emotionally impacted anxiety situations, or activities carried over from the previous day; (2) current emotionally impacted conscious wishes that refuse to be forgotten during sleep but clamor for their fulfillment.

My husband often has a typical mild anxiety dream that is a residue of the previous day. I feel sorry for him when he talks and tosses during these dreams, for he might as well be in the sales field working hard. If he happens to remember these dreams the next day, I can find no ESP value in them, for his dream task has not been brought to a conclusion. If a person who has native dream ESP, or one who has trained the dream faculty successfully, dreams of a work that is either accomplished satisfactorily or that fails, he can expect to accomplish a current project or fail to do so, whichever way his dream portends. But the work-work no-conclusion type of dream such as my husband experiences is merely a meandering of the preconscious through recent work memories. It is hard to find value of any kind in rest-disturbing dreams of this nature.

And when we come into the consideration of emotionally impacted wish-fulfilling ego dreams, there is again a defeat of ESP factors. If such a dream coincides with a happy resolution of the anxiety that produced it, we must ascribe it to chance, not to ESP. And all too often such dreams are the opposite of the happy resolution portrayed, as the following dream will illustrate.

The Lost Dog Dream. Years ago, when my daughter was still a child, her dog disappeared. A few nights later she dreamed that she once again held the little pet in her arms. Alas, it was not to be. Despite our efforts we were never able to obtain a clue concerning the fate of the dog. Influenced by intense emotion, my daughter's ego had reacted by influencing a *simple wish fulfillment*, not a production of ESP.

The person who wishes important questions answered must beware of desires he has carried over into the dream state in such a manifest content that there are no associative possibilities or no symbols that must be looked up in dream books. In such instances, the ego may be doing a bit of daydreaming at night. A man making the navy his career had his heart set on achieving a higher commission. After taking a test for this advancement, he always dreamed that he had passed. Finally, after the fourth test and the fourth dream of victory, he did pass. It is doubtful that any of these dreams, even the fourth, were paranormal productions.

But the following example presents a similar situation in which the final two dreams might have been paranormal. Again, we have a case history of a man seeking promotion in the navy who kept dreaming that he had been made a chief. Finally, after a long series of flunking tests, or passing and not being appointed, the man took a final test that he was sure he flunked. This conviction caused him to lose interest in the navy as a career, and he decided to retire. But when he began to look forward to civilian life, he dreamed two nights in succession that he had been made a chief. Soon, to his great surprise, he was promoted.

According to an old folklore belief, when a wish is dreamed of favorably for two nights it will come to pass. For the sake of research, I hope my readers will send me examples of successive simple wish-fulfillment dreams and their outcome.

However, in the case under discussion, I am sure that if there was actual ESP in the two successive dreams, it was able to occur because there was no longer a conscious emotional bias.

But it is difficult to lay down rules that apply to all people in regard to the ESP value of emotionally impacted simple wish fulfillment dreams. And it is also difficult to make a correct decision, in some instances, as to whether or not an emotionally impacted dream may have paranormal value. For example, I once knew a man who was caught in a love triangle involving a plain but brilliant wife away at college and a flamboyant, ardent girl. When he dreamed that he told his wife about the new romantic interest, she did not react with the rage and tears he had expected. Instead, she was very understanding, even nonchalant, making it clear that she would not prohibit her husband's association with the younger, prettier woman when she went back to school. The man was extremely puzzled by this dream, for it had never occurred to him that his jealous wife could act so entirely out of character.

When this dream came true in surprising detail, I sought out the factors that made it possible. In the first place, the dreamer was a man with a high ESP quotient. In the second place, the dream was an emotionally impacted simple wish fulfillment only to a degree. The man's full-fledged desire—to have his wife ask for a divorce—was not granted, either in the dream or in waking life.

The partial wish fulfillment of the above dream reminds me of another dream in which the wish for the recovery of a sick little cat was partially granted for just a short term before the death of the cat—a foreshadowing of what fate had in store. The events leading up to this dream are as follows.

One day I managed to capture a kitten that had been born to a wild stray for whom I was in the habit of setting out food. The little fellow adjusted well to owning and training me, but even the best food, care, and vitamins failed to make him strong. Every three or four weeks he would come down with a fever and a partially comatose condition that the veterinarian said would one day prove fatal. One evening after the veterinarian's office had closed, this kitten became so very ill that I decided the kindest thing I could do for him was to take him in the next day for the release of euthanasia.

Later that evening I entertained some of my husband's business associates, serving them margaritas in sherbet glasses. That night I had the following dream.

The Little Sick Cat Dream. I dreamed I was looking at a tiny caricature of a cat, no bigger than a bumble bee, that was trying to struggle up the sides of a sherbet glass to the rim. He was an odd little cat, indeed, for he had no fur but looked as though he had been cut out of a piece of bright red paper. He struggled and slid, struggled and slid, in his efforts to reach the top of the glass, and finally he succeeded. I turned to my husband happily. "I think the little cat will make it," I said. "I think he will live." As soon as I finished speaking, the cat slipped from his perch on the rim of the glass and fell to the floor where he became nothing but a tiny pool of red blood.

The next morning the little cat had perked up so much that my husband was loathe to take him to the veterinarian. I agreed happily. "I think the little cat will make it. I think he will live!" The words had a familiar sound, and in a flash I remembered having spoken them in my dream. During the day the little cat gained more strength and even became a bit playful. But the next morning we found him dead. Beside him on the den floor was a little pool of bright red blood he had spit up.

I am inclined to believe that the ESP determinant was able to operate efficiently in the *Little Sick Cat Dream* because the coming fact of an impermanent recovery could be substituted to gratify the wish fulfillment for a full and permanent recovery. When the wish was thus gratified, emotional pull was defeated and the death of the cat could then be predicted.

In some instances, the ESP determinant is able to outwit an emotionally impacted conscious wish by presenting its subject matter and then substituting another wish that provides a truthful answer. The following dream is an example of this principle.

The Returned Manuscript Dream. I went to the mailbox where I found a large manila envelope. Upon opening it, I discovered three copies of the same manuscript. "Why three copies?" I wondered. "They were supposed to return only two." Then I burst into a torrent of tears.

The main question on my mind, at the time of this dream, was whether or not a certain manuscript I had submitted to the New York Parapsychology Foundation would win a prize. A short time after this dream, I went to my mailbox and picked up a large manila envelope that I thought contained two originals of one of my articles that had been published by a magazine featuring the paranormal. For a few seconds I found myself wondering, "Why three copies? I sent only two." Then I realized that the manuscript copies I was looking at were the ones submitted in the hope of winning the prize. I did not cry when I read the slip telling me I had not won, for the dream had prepared me and I am not the kind who cries over spilled milk.

In this instance, I think the ESP determinants of the dream had outwitted a residue wish fulfillment portrayal by granting an old wish to cry. When I was little, my mother did not allow me to wash away small frustrations with the torrents of tears that are so natural to childhood. The tears in this dream were not of grief. They seemed to be a release. Nevertheless, there was a second level of prophecy connected with these tears. I wanted the prize money for a friend, and when she passed away, I could not think of her for a long time without tears.

In another dream, the simple residue wish, which was not too emotionally impacted, both forwarded and impeded the

ESP content. This dream is one of the favorites of my collection for it had realistically true features, the dream *material* being material in the sense that is the most common and literal to me—dress material.

The Dream of the Little Shirts. I went to my clothes closet where I found three size two baby shirts on pink and blue children's clothes hangers. As I handled the little shirts, they became so outstanding that I could "feel" their textures most realistically. A little bright yellow shirt was made of nylon knit. Another shirt was a poplin, a deep orange with white polka dots. The third shirt was a vivid blue organdy. In the dream I was happy to find these shirts, for I would have the pleasure of giving them to my grandson.

When I woke up, I realized the absurd features of this dream. My grandson was three years old and far too big for size two baby shirts. He was so large for his age that all baby hangers had been taken out of his wardrobe closet and replaced with the adult size. And, of course, little boys' shirts are not cut from nylon knit, poplin, or organdy materials.

The day after this dream I went shopping, intent upon giving myself the pleasure of buying books for my little grandson. However, on my way to the book section of a large department store, I bumped into a rack of sale-priced dresses for little girls. My granddaughter was only nine months old at the time, but since I knew she would soon grow into the smallest of the dresses, I decided to buy as many as I could. Other women were snatching at the dresses, but I managed to find three that were only size two. While I waited my turn at the cashier's station, I examined the dresses and found myself back in my dream of the night before. One dress was a bright yellow nylon knit. The second was an orange-colored poplin with white polka dots, and the third was a vivid blue organdy! Each dress was on a pink and blue infant size clothes hanger!

I am convinced that the realistically true features of this dream resulted from a week's reinforcement of certain associations with a wish that was not emotional. I had been ill the entire week before my shopping spree. During that time, I lay upon my bed, often staring at an open closet that revealed clothing of various colors and materials (but not the colors and materials of the baby shirts in the dream) that hung upon clothes hangers. And often I comforted myself with the promise that as soon as the last symptoms of fever, chill, and nausea so common to influenza had subsided, I should give myself the pleasure of shopping for books for my grandson whose mind was developing so thrillingly. I did not think of shopping for my granddaughter, for at nine months she did not have the agile mind that so charms me today.

But although this dream had been triggered by a simple ego wish of the residue type, this same wish deflects from a completely true precognitive presentation, for it caused me to dream of shirts for a little boy instead of dresses for a little girl.

Not all emotional pull in divinatory work is toward the heart's desire. Occasionally, fear can defeat the ESP determinant. For instance, a mother may so fear that her child will run into the street and be hit by an automobile that the dread of such a situation can be reflected in a terrible ego dream. Such anxiety dreams should not be confused with id dreams that carry out a death wish. I have had so few anxiety dreams of this nature that I can recall only one in which a deep sense of disappointment defeated the ESP determinant. The following dream occurred in 1971 at a time when the coming 1972 election was on my mind.

The Election Dream. I made my way to the outdoor theater of a park for I knew an important event was being celebrated there. A band was playing and American flags were flying. Beneath these flags stood Senator Muskie happily receiving congratulations for having been elected to the presidency of the United States.

In the dream, I was both bitterly bewildered and deeply

disappointed, just as would have been the case in waking life. Although I admired Senator Muskie, I was a Republican and I felt that President Nixon had achieved so much for the country that I wanted him to continue in office.

My political dreams have always been so accurate that I was tempted to register the prediction of a Senator Muskie presidential victory with the Central Premonitions Bureau in New York. But I did not do so because I was wary of the strong emotion I had experienced during the dream. A short time later, I had a dream that corrected the situation.

The Nixon Victory Dream. I was back in grade school doing monitor duty in one of the hallways. Somewhere in the building a band began to play "Hail to the Chief," and I heard marching feet. As these sounds gained in intensity, I knew that the band and the marchers who followed it would soon arrive in the hallway in which I stood. Another monitor ran up to me and placed a large American flag on a long pole in my hands. "Quick!" he shouted. "The next president of the United States is coming! Fling open the front doors, then stand to the right with the flag unfurled. A large crowd is out there."

In that instant I noticed I was dressed only in a pink slip. What an outfit in which to perform a public ceremony for a newly elected president! But there was nothing I could do, for the victorious president, whom I couldn't see clearly, was already in the upper hallway just ahead of the band. I grabbed the flag, ran to the two front doors, and flung them open. Then, unfurling the flag, I marched to the side of the right door and stood smartly at attention as President Nixon swept by to greet the cheering crowd.

I felt no great elation in this dream as was to be the case when President Nixon actually won the 1972 election. My emotions were too involved with my embarrassment for my scanty clothing and my relief that the crowd was too charmed by the president to pay attention to my predicament.

When I woke up and analyzed this dream, I realized it was partially of the ego and partially of the id. I theorized that the ego portion, which was a simple wish fulfillment, was no doubt true for it was without emotion. Evidently the ESP determinant had routed all emotion into feelings of embarrassment by clothing me inadequately in the id portion. In Chapter 11, I shall have more to say about these exhibitionist id dreams and the way the ESP component handles them.

It is possible for the ESP determinant to present predictions without using a substitute wish or deflecting the emotional content away from the wish as was perhaps the case in the *Nixon Victory Dream*. In some instances a wish entertained during waking hours with considerable feeling can be gratified in a dream in which no emotion is felt. And when the mind is trained to dream true, these dreams are often highly accurate. The following case will serve as an illustration of this statement.

My feelings toward Senator Edward Kennedy at the time of a dream in 1970 were that he was too young to assume the presidency of the United States. Because I knew that Senator Kennedy was the Democrat who might possibly beat President Nixon, I planned to process his chances through the cards. However, at that time the election was two years away, and I decided not to work on this issue until January of 1972. As it happened, I was too busy in 1972 to do any divinatory work regarding the election. Perhaps this dream and my *Nixon Victory Dream* came early because my subconscious knew my mind would be on other matters during election year.

The Edward Kennedy Headline Dream. I was trying to read the headlines of a newspaper. I knew they were about Senator Edward Kennedy but the lines were blurred. Then a voice intoned a rhyme: "It's too bad he didn't run. He could have won."

During this dream I felt no emotion whatsoever. But when

the senator announced in real life that he would not run, I felt relieved and happy, for I knew President Nixon had escaped his maximum competition.

Chapter Summary

When evaluating the ESP content of ego dreams, we must often deal with emotion as it operates on two levels: (1) in waking life; (2) in the dream experience. The first dream presented, the *Lost Dog Dream*, is heavily emotional on both levels, the happy outcome of the dream being nothing more than an outright wish fulfillment. Also, waking anxiety situations or a consciously entertained fear can be transferred to a dream at the expense of ESP. The *Election Dream* is an example of a conscious fear being carried over into the dream state.

Fortunately, the ESP determinant has ways of defeating emotional influence during a dream in the ways listed below, and there may also be other methods:

1.   By waiting until the real life emotion concerning a matter has subsided, as may have been the case with the second dream example of a petty officer dreaming he had been promoted to chief.

2.   By channeling wish fulfillment energy into a partial wish fulfillment that is to take place in real life and then depicting the disappointing aspect. The *Little Sick Cat Dream* is an example.

3.   By presenting the subject matter of an emotional situation and then substituting another wish to supply the answer. An example of this method is the *Returned Manuscript Dream*.

4.   By presenting a dream such as the *Nixon Victory Dream* which evades emotional pull by channeling energy into a more engrossing situation.

5.   By managing to escape emotion that can be expected to carry over from waking life to the dream state. The *Kennedy Headline Dream* is an example of this strategy.

6.   By managing to use a simple wish to structure a prediction that is at least partially true concerning a related matter, as was the case in the *Dream of the Little Shirts*. (This dream may also indicate that a simple wish is a good structure for ESP when it has been entertained for several days in an environment affording association with a coming event related to the wish.)

I have reason to believe that when the dream faculty is trained there are fewer emotionally impacted simple wish fulfillment dreams that defeat ESP. There are usually more dreams—often id tinged, which must be deciphered through association or code—that are able to evade emotional pull and provide a correct interpretation. Though the ego dreams I have presented in this chapter are interestingly complex in their range and scope, the novice at parapsychological dream interpretation has only one simple rule to follow: Pay attention to the danger sign I have posted along the paths of the dream world. Do not place faith in the ego dream that is directly emotionally favorable to a current highly emotional desire. Usually the only good thing about these dreams is that, when they are favorable, they may come true. According to the laws of probability theory, there is about a fifty-fifty chance that has nothing to do, in most cases, with ESP.

There is, I think, only one dependable exception to the above rule—the *Informative Dream*. On occasion, when we or a loved one are facing a seemingly unsolvable problem or a great danger, the ESP determinant responds by presenting an ego dream that tells us exactly what to do to clear the formidable situation under which we are laboring. In Chapter 15 I shall present an informative dream that enabled me to save my son from a terminal disease and bring him back to health and well being.

9

The ESP Content
of Jungian Dreams

Before I can deal with Jung's genius in the area of dreams, and before I can relate his findings to the ESP content of our nocturnal productions, I must reveal the block that was his weakness in dream interpretation—his inability to recognize the psychological facts of life regarding the Electra-Oedipus complexes—a fear of self-revelation so great that, more often than not, he closed his eyes to the set Freudian sex symbols.

Because he was a physician, Jung knew there is much in the physiology of man that is of necessity ugly, such as the sewage system of the bladder and the bowels. But even though the main study of his life was devoted to the theory of the *collective unconscious*, and its atavistic influences carried over from the lower animals and prehistoric man, sensitivity to the nature of his own affliction made it difficult for him to realize that the unconscious must also deal with waste products that relate to the tendency of man and animals toward incest, a practice that was discarded only as man came to realize its harm for the race. No one knew better than symbol-conscious Jung that parental incest—with its death wish for the parent of the opposite sex—is so strong a component of the unconscious that it is reflected in the cultural products of every race, insinuating its prohibited desire, time after time, into myths, religious rites, folktales, pageants, and dreams. Although he admitted that incest is an archetype, he reduced it to a sporadic pathological symptom that is not relevant to general psychology.

Jung could not dispense with the Oedipus-Electra complexes entirely and still maintain an effective discipline of analysis and therapy. He solved this dilemma by relegating all traces of incestuous evidence in dreams to a mere desire to return to childhood. Only the protection of the parent of the opposite sex is wanted. Sex does not enter the picture even in the mildest form. While there are many instances of "perverted" children, there is no general period of infantile sexuality either consciously or subconsciously.

This compromise with Freudian psychology meant that Jung had to make an adjustment in dream analysis. While admitting there is a simple wish fulfillment in some dreams, Jung refuted the theory of a *latent* wish fulfillment. The latent content is never in the dream itself, but only in the dreamer's interpretation. Therefore, the fixed sex symbols are never regarded as such unless they are accompanied by an open reference to sex or are interpreted by the dreamer himself as having a sexual connotation.

The folly of doing away with latent wish fulfillment and the actual meanings of sex symbols, as such, during the treatment of a neurosis, is naively disclosed by Jung himself, who related the following bungled analysis in his book, *Modern Man in Search of a Soul*. The patient in this case was a young woman who submitted dreams, similar in content, to three different analysts, the third being Jung.

In the first dream, the patient had to cross the frontier to a foreign country, but she could not find the way. The analysis was too slow to suit the young patient, and so she went to a second analyst to whom she presented dream number two in which she had to cross a frontier but could not find the customs office because it was dark. In her efforts to find her way, she had to cross a valley and a deep wood. Then she was joined by someone who "grasped her like a madman," and she awakened in terror. But again, patient and physician were not compatible, and the patient then came to Jung.

This patient must have been contemplating marriage when she visited the first two analysts because she married while consulting Jung, but without telling him. She did, however, tell him the following dream. She had crossed a frontier and was in a customs house where she thought she had "nothing to declare." But the customs official dived into her bag and pulled out two mattresses.

According to Jung's own admission it took him eighteen months to discover, by some roundabout way he does not disclose, that his patient's trouble was related to a deep-seated resistance to marriage. He insisted that there was no hint of this in the above three dreams! They meant only that the first two analysts would be unsuccessful whereas he would succeed. This interpretation was true on the predictive level but had little to do with the patient's problems.

A Freudian analyst would have gotten to the root of the neurosis at once. In the first place, crossing a frontier in a dream means a contemplated change in the life of the dreamer. Supplied with this clue, a Freudian analyst would have at once queried into the life of the patient to ascertain what change she had in mind. In fact, most Freudians know that a neurosis often crops up just before or after an important change, and they obtain such information before the analysis begins. The fact that the dreamer cannot find the frontier means there is a subconscious wish not to make the change, regardless of how ardently she may desire it consciously. The fixed sex symbols in the second dream are the trees, which on the psychological level can represent the pubic hair of either sex; and the general dream terrain, the anatomy of the opposite sex. These sex symbols are reinforced by the "someone" who "joins" the patient in the dream and clings to her, a wish fulfillment that is punished by the superego or some masochistic or chemical tendency that so often inflicts punishment, even in latent sex dreams.

The two telltale mattresses that are found in the possession of the dreamer in the third dream—even though she "thought she had nothing to declare"—represent two repressed sex episodes that might have occurred early in the life of the dreamer. Either this, or they represent infantile sex fantasies of the kind that so often come to light, during analysis, to reveal the incestuous longings entertained during childhood and then forgotten.

In spite of his shortcomings, Jung did have great insight regarding dreamers and their dreams. Every person, according to Jung, has a subconscious archetype called the *shadow*, which is reflected in our culture, especially in conventional religion, as the devil. And the shadow is devilishly complex. He consists mainly of everything we have considered bad or evil and have tried to repress. But that which we have considered evil may be so only in our opinion, and the shadow is also compounded of *good* qualities we have failed to develop. According to the Jungian psychologists, the shadow always appears in our dreams as a person of our own sex, usually a stranger. If you dream of an uncouth person of your own sex, or one who is morally lax or a cheat, you may be receiving a dream warning not to let your shadow take possession of you. But if you dream of a stranger of your own sex who displays courage, chivalry, or any other virtue, you may be viewing desirable traits that are lacking in your makeup and that should be developed.

Among the hundreds of dreams submitted to me, I have

seldom detected a shadow—possibly because I move among psychics whose dreams are more pointed toward ESP than to psychology—but the following is one example from my experience.

The dreamer was a good friend of mine, a woman in her late sixties who had been charmingly broadminded and jolly until the onset of a serious disease that made her extremely critical and sometimes even hostile. One day she called me on the telephone to tell me she was sure she would not die because she had had the following dream.

The Naughty Actress Dream. She was a pupil in a college class that was being disrupted by a well-known actress whose name I won't bother to mention. The teacher, a man, pointed to a sign over the door that said *Death*, and he told the actress she must leave the room. Then he made it a point to tell the dreamer that she did not have to pass through the door. As the actress flounced petulantly out of the room, the dreamer remarked, "Well! That's the end of her!"

The actress is still alive, but my ailing friend passed away three weeks later. The dream is a source of comfort to me, for I interpret it to mean that only the *shadow* of my friend had to die in the final sense, and that she is now her charming self on the other side of life. It has been noted by some dream authorities that actors of the same sex as ourselves often represent the way we are acting.

Even Jungians admit that Jungian dreams are rare. In most of the dreams that come to my attention, a stranger of the same sex as the dreamer who portrays a fault is not the shadow of the dreamer but another person who will prove difficult in real life. But, as I have stated before, perhaps this situation is especially true for those dreamers who have trained their dreams to be predictive. Here is an example of what I mean.

A student of mine had started a spiritual meditation class in her own home. Then she dreamed that she and several other women were cleaning a church, but as they swept dirt out, another woman littered the floor with trash. The dream was predictive, for a newcomer joined the meditation group and tried to reduce it to the level of gossip sessions.

At one time I wanted a reading from a well-known psychic, but I was afraid to go to her because I had heard she often refused to read for other psychics. That night I had a dream in which one character became dimensional as the rest of the dream faded out. A woman who had a doll's face beneath a head of white hair smiled at me warmly. The medium was more than gracious when she received me. She was a "doll." She also had the regularity of features one sees in a doll, and her facial expression, like a doll's, was rather set due to several face lifts. In this dream the stranger of my own sex was not my shadow reflecting undeveloped qualities. Though I know there are good qualities toward which I should make an effort, warmth toward others is characteristic of me.

In closing the subject of the shadow, I believe the concept to be more valid in dreams of strangers of the same sex who are either criticized by others for their bad qualities or praised for their good qualities. In both instances, the inner mind may be issuing a warning to the dreamer, either to overcome negative characteristics or to live up to the full potential of the better self. Also, examine your dreams to ascertain whether or not they consistently portray strangers of the same sex as yourself who are either decidedly superior or inferior to you. In both instances, you are no doubt receiving a warning to take yourself in hand.

For a period of time my dreams were often filled with women who were strangers to me—bystanders who had nothing to do with me or the issues with which I was concerned. These strangers were always women younger than I who glowed with good health. More than this, invariably they were modishly dressed and impeccably groomed. I had not had my hair styled since reaching the age of fifty, some years before these dreams set in. I had become so intensely interested in psychic research and getting my findings before the world that the only attention I gave myself most days was a quick shower, two daily stints with a toothbrush, a dash of lipstick, and a comb run through my hair. Often I was too interested in what I was doing to take time out for vitamins, exercise, or proper diet. At night, I forgot the clock and continued my research until two or three o'clock in the morning.

In spite of this over-drive and neglect, I wished for a long lifespan, for my work is fascinating and so much remains to be done. Making an effort to solve this conflict, my dream faculty was trying to tell me, via my shadow, that if I wished to "stay young" and live longer, I must take care of myself as the women in my dreams were so obviously doing. It was only by making such women repetitive in my dreams that I could be taught this lesson. From the standpoint of both psychology and parapsychology, it is interesting to note that as soon as I "got the message," these do-nothing bystanders ceased appearing in my dreams. No, I did not resolve to spend hours of my precious time grooming myself, for I knew this was not the lesson my dreams were trying to teach, but I did begin to take care of myself with a healthful daily routine. It is also interesting to note that my shadow bystanders neither forwarded nor impeded the ESP content of the dreams in which they appeared.

It has been my happy observation that when the dream faculty is trained toward ESP, a dreamer's faults are often revealed in more forthright ways than is the case in shadow depictions. This adjustment allows more leeway for the ESP determinant to let erring dream characters stand for themselves in the predictive sense.

A student of mine, a bookkeeper, dreamed that two children got into the office cashbox and got it "all mixed up." A Jungian expert interpreted this dream to mean that my student was, herself, "childishly mixed up." I could not agree with this interpretation, for my student is well organized in all departments of life. Three days later, while she was out to lunch, her employer allowed his two children to play with the cashbox and to help themselves to some change and dollar bills. Need I add that these children got the cashbox "all mixed up"?

Regarding methods more forthright than the shadow in depicting a dreamer's character faults, I shall give more details of this phenomenon in the next chapter when I give consideration to the moralistic aspects of the Great Dreams discovered by Jung.

Two of Jung's most interesting archetypes are the *anima* and the *animus*. Those who are male have repressed female tendencies that constitute the *anima*, whereas females have repressed male tendencies that form the *animus*. When the anima takes possession of a man, he may find himself rendered passive, illogical, or tearful. When the animus gains the upper hand in a woman's psyche, she is apt to become coldly dogmatic and critical, forgetting to temper these pronouncements with judgment, restraint, and mercy. Often the anima or animus becomes tinged by the shadow because we have repressed as "bad" those tendencies towards characteristics of the other sex. Such a mingling of the shadow with the animus or anima is unfortunate, for we tend to identify, when we fall in love, with our own repressed male or female tendencies and to seek them out in our mates. This is why we sometimes see a man of good character married to a woman who is flighty and shallow, or an idealistic woman hopelessly attracted to a rakish or abusive man.

Whenever the anima appears in a man's dreams, she is, of course, always a female. Conversely, when a woman views her animus in a dream, it is always a male. Frequently, because the anima is shadow-tinged, she will often appear in a man's dreams as a dangerous woman, often one who is a dark foreigner. And when the animus appears in a woman's dreams, he, too, is often a dangerous, quite dark foreigner.

It has been pointed out as a psychological fact that students of Jungian psychology are apt to have more Jungian than Freudian dreams, and that those studying Freud are more apt to dream in the Freudian than in the Jungian style. After studying Jung, I had the following two animus dreams.

The Violated Virgin Dream I. I am again a school girl in my early teens. My dress is simple, but white and lace trimmed. As I stand before a mirror, I weave garlands of white blossoms into my hair and I am happy to note they enhance my face, which is devoid of makeup. Turning away from the mirror, I start to walk down a wide hallway (the hallway of a school I once attended). I experience a thrill of elated expectancy and feel that something wonderful is about to happen to me. Instead, a very brutish dark youth comes up to me and twists my arm until I wake myself up with a cry of pain.

The Violated Virgin Dream II. Within a few minutes, I am back asleep and once again wearing the white dress of the first dream, and I still have the same white flowers in my hair. I am still in the hallway of the school, but this time I am standing in an open doorway. Just outside the door, the dark youth of my first dream is working beneath a car. My attitude toward the hard-working dark youth is both resentful and triumphant. "This is your punishment," I state smugly. "You must work to support me all the days of your life!"

To any Jungian dream analyst, these two dreams indicate that I am on very bad terms with my animus. But if this were the case, I don't see how I could have chosen a mate so compatible to my nature as my husband, or how I could have lived so happily with my blond, blue-eyed mate (not a mechanic but a business executive most of our married life) for thirty-seven years. And while I do believe that a woman should choose a mate who is able to support her and their children, like most modern wives I have willingly contributed my own wage-earning efforts whenever this was necessary. This part of the dream must have been atavistic to a time when support by a male was a necessity to a marriage.

I am sure that Jungian dreams experienced during a Jungian analysis are more accurate in revealing the dreamer's relationship to the animus or the anima than the dream I have just recounted, for I think my dream was more an association with my Jungian reading than an accurate depiction of my animus status.

Dreams have several different levels of content; in my first Jungian animus dream, do we not also encounter Freud's latent wish fulfillment? When using the slang expression "you twisted my arm," we mean we have been talked into something we really wished to do in the first place. And when the symbols of virginity—the white dress and the white blossoms —are violated, does not the censor step in? The second dream grants a wish fulfillment for marriage, for it indicates a lifetime support through the efforts of a husband. Since the wish in this dream had long since been fulfilled in waking life, it is little more than an activation of a wish that was on my mind during my school days.

I shall next detail two animus dreams that were highly predictive, but first I must present their most unusual psychic background. Because much happens here in San Diego, I often use this city as an ESP target. By programming my "Associative Card Code," I have been able, over a period of years, to predict the calendar quarters when we were to experience tidal wave alerts or earthquakes. And in some instances, I have been able to pinpoint the intensity of an earthquake as well as the quarter of the year in which it would occur. For instance, I once predicted that the next earthquake would measure between five and six points on the Richter scale. When the earthquake occurred, in the quarter of the year I said it would, it measured 5.2.

But the San Diego prediction that caused me the most

concern was a message in the cards, in 1968, telling me that San Diego would be involved in an attack by the military of a foreign power. I worked to pinpoint the time in the cards and decided the attack would occur in November. Then I sent a Western Union telegram to record the prediction with the Central Premonitions Bureau in New York. While I was working with the cards to ascertain the safety of myself and my friends, and also to determine from what country the attack would come, a pupil of mine programmed herself to dream the answers.

This pupil's next dream was that her eight-year-old daughter was raped by "a swarthy dark man with an oily skin." The dreamer comforted her daughter, telling her that she wasn't hurt and that her life wasn't ruined. Here the shadow-tinged animus accomplishes the rape that the dreamer wanted for herself, but the censor uses an old trick by *displacing* persons. In waking life, the dreamer, a woman in her prime, was neglected by her husband. There is little wonder that she wished, subconsciously, for a stranger (the foreigner in her dream) to take her by force.

The second dream of the night makes this wish quite clear. In this dream, the same swarthy, oily-skinned stranger chased the dreamer down a hallway. She jumped into a swiftly ascending elevator (a sex-act symbol), but she did not elude her pursuer. He was in the elevator. She pushed a button marked *Panic*, and the elevator came to a stop at the top floor where she managed to make her escape.

When the last day of November arrived, I thought the prediction had been a miss. But that night as I watched television a bulletin was flashed on the screen. A Mexican man-of-war had shot across the bow of one of San Diego's tuna ships, and our entire Coast Guard was being alerted. Frantic hotline messages flew between America and Mexico until the incident was classified as a military mistake on the part of Mexico.

The dreams of my student had indeed answered her

questions. The animus, in this case, represented a Mexican. While the first dream reveals that the foreseen attack won't hurt or "ruin" anyone, the second reveals an escape from the threatened danger.

10

The ESP Content of Great Dreams

One of Jung's greatest contributions was his recognition and classification of Great Dreams. Even Freud had some respect for the accumulation of "big" dreams that appear in the history of man and in the files of researchers. And though he did not accord them a full prophetic value, he did not dismiss them as being worthless as prognostications. However, as he states in his *Interpretation of Dreams*, he felt that the science of psychology was not at that time ready to deal with dreams as they might relate to future events. Freud's analytical processes were so highly organized that they bordered on intuition. He was right in his conclusion that a serious study of the prophetic element in dreams—for which their proclivity toward condensation might allow room—had best be postponed until their psychological functioning was fully understood. My own findings prove that all elements of the dream, including those that were later to be isolated by Jung, are used by the ESP determinant.

113

One of these elements, usually attributed to Jung, was revealed to Jung in a dream in which he saw a house of two stories over a basement. Under this house lay subterranean vault after subterranean vault, finally ending in a cave cluttered with the skulls and artifacts of a primitive culture.

Fortified by this dream, Jung began to lecture and write on the theory he named the *collective unconscious*. However, Freud had referred to this theory earlier as *archaic remnants*. In fact, it was so vital to Freud's system of psychoanalysis and diagnosis that he had commissioned a research collaborator to seek out recurring themes in myths, fairy tales, and folklore and to publish these findings in book form.

After his break with Freud, Jung suffered another breakdown during which he withdrew from his practice for a period of self-analysis. He emerged from this illness with a philosophy he considered new but that bore the markings of the Oedipus complex that was to haunt him all the days of his life. However, he *had* gained the advantage of some breakthrough knowledge concerning the collective unconscious that he could call his own, such as the archetypes that were discussed in the previous chapter. These ominous and universal symbols, which relate intimately to both man and his environment, opened the door to still another discovery—*Great Dreams*.

Because Jung's second neurotic bout had been signaled by an obsession to draw mandalas—the integration of concentric designs into forms, usually of a circular or elliptical scheme—Jung believed that his psyche was endeavoring to integrate his personality into the "complete self." This theory, which has had backing in the symbology and rites of many cultures, is based upon the perception of the mandala as the cosmos with its central point from which all is radiated and into which all must be drawn.

Jung knew that the unconscious processes that were compelling him to draw mandalas also had to be at work in his dreams, which he recorded and analyzed thoroughly. Yes, it was true. Some dreams amount to far more than mere depictions of psychological functioning. They are meaningful and helpful in a far broader sense, affording guidance intended to help us make constructive personality adjustments, or to meet a crisis successfully, or to understand ourselves more fully.

All of the Great Dreams contain archetypes. I have discussed three of these archetypes in the previous chapter—the shadow, symbolized by the devil, the anima in a man, and the animus in a woman. These archetypes find expression in our dreams and other creative efforts. There are many other archetypes that are not personality components but themes in nature and the life experience of the race that are repetitive in a common imagery. Among these archetypes are: the *hero* who wins great treasure after facing struggle and danger; the *great mother*, who symbolizes both "Mother Nature" and the human mother; the *wise old man* who represents wisdom and prudence; the *magician*, representative of procreation and other acts of creation; and the *egg*, the symbol of the world.

Even the Great Dreams usually have a Freudian substructure. Nothing amuses me more than Jungian experts who go into print with dreams in which they defy the reader to find an expression of Freudian wish fulfillment. With the exception of anxiety dreams, and sometimes even in these, I have always been able to find the Freudian wish fulfillment in published Jungian dreams. And so, in recounting the first Great Dream to be presented in this chapter, I shall give an object lesson in appraising the Great Dreams at their full value, for even dreams that lead to personal development have elements structured upon Freudian psychological factors.

This dream has an interesting background. A friend of mine had developed outstanding psychic ability that she wished to dedicate to helping others. Although she was highly spiritual, she had a pronounced tendency to criticize and scold those who came to her for counseling, a personality flaw that

Jung would classify as an animus possession. A friend of hers who was a Jungian expert wanted her to discover this problem for herself, and so did I, but we did not know what to do until a dream solved the problem.

The Beautifully Colored Egg Dream. The psychic arose from her bed and went to her window where she beheld hundreds of horses all of which seemed pale and sickly or deformed. Leaving the window, she went up a flight of stairs. Seating herself at the top of the stairway, she laid a "beautifully colored egg." Then she descended the stairs and went back to the window. To her amazement, the horses, though still pale in color, were now strong and healthy. More than this, they were "thrillingly beautiful."

Upon awakening, the dreamer immediately telephoned the friend who had made a depth study of Jungian dream theory. He told her the horses represented people, of whom she was generally too critical. The ascension of the stairs represented her pride. The laying of the egg was a compound depiction of the *great mother* creating a beautiful world, symbolized by the egg, and the dreamer's wish to remake the world. The act of descending the stairs represented a desire to acquire humility, a state that would enable the dreamer to help make others whole by finding and strengthening their good qualities instead of dwelling on their faults. She would then find that people are basically as wholesome and beautiful as the transformed horses in her dream.

After hearing this version of her dream, the psychic then came to me for my interpretation. She was amazed when I evaluated the content, point by point, in accord with the Jungian expert. Then she expressed the Jungian egg symbol in terms of a Freudian play upon words: "I 'laid an egg' in my counseling. I shall try never again to attempt to help people by pointing out all their faults."

There is also a Freudian structure in this dream, leading to an ESP content that can only be understood by knowledge of certain facts in the dreamer's life. In her church, the psychic, who was a woman in her forties, had met a young black man whose devotion to Jesus gave him the unselfish ideal of living for others at the expense of his own personal desires. A strong attachment sprang up between the dreamer and this man that manifested in him only as friendship, but in her it was a desire for a total relationship in the marital state. Subconsciously, at least, she wanted a child as a final tie to her love. In the dream, the sex act is accomplished (her ascension of the stairs), and so is her desired parturition (laying the "beautifully colored egg"). But then she descends the stairs, always an ESP dream signal that a desired purpose will not be accomplished. However, when she again looks out her window, the horses (symbols of the sex drive that often represent men in the dreams of women) are no longer undesirable to her, but in her own words "thrillingly beautiful."

The ESP content of this dream is that the dreamer will recover from her love, which is unreturned, and once again see desirable traits in other men.

The full-range possibilities of man's dream faculty can be likened to the piano keyboard. The compositions it can express are based upon the lower tones of Freudian psychology, the middle notes of ESP, and the higher octaves of personality development and spiritual rebirth.

The trouble with the moral guidance in dreams such as the above is that they are so disguised in content that the dreamer seldom perceives the lesson they contain. I greatly prefer the forthright, easily understood lesson dreams that come to me now that my mind is trained. When I am in the wrong in a situation, I often dream that my stepfather or some authoritative male figure is giving me a good scolding. When I wake up, I see the matter in its true perspective and set it straight. At other times, my superego may set me straight with a dream of a scolding over a telephone, or by letter. On other occasions, symbols in a dream book give me moral guidance or tell me how to improve myself, as illustrated in the following example.

We are all inclined to be a bit interfering and bossy, at times, under the rationalization that these actions are not for personal satisfaction but in the best interests of others. At one time, I was tempted to interfere with a family of friends in a matter that did not concern me. Fortunately, I dreamed that I walked along a path bordered by a certain flower. My dream book told me that this flower is a signal for the dreamer to mind his own business, and, rather reluctantly, I accepted the message. Later, I learned that the family was under expert psychological counseling, which I could have bungled with my own opinions had I stepped in at that time.

Although not all Great Dreams are moralistic, they, too, can give guidance. Great Dreams can help us through a time of crisis, either in a present situation or one to be experienced later in life. Here is the situation leading up to a Great Dream that saved my husband's sanity and perhaps even his life several years after the dream occurred.

At the time of this dream, my husband was facing a major life change—he was about to marry a grey-eyed girl named Thelma whom he loved dearly. My husband is a Latter-Day Saint, or Mormon, among whom marriage is the greatest covenant and sacrament—a "sealing," not just until death, but throughout all eternity in a pact in which each party is essential to the other's highest salvation. One day, a few weeks before his marriage, my husband returned home from work, kissed his mother happily, and bounded up the stairs to change his clothes. But as soon as he closed his bedroom door, a strange drowsiness, unnatural to the hour of the day, assailed him. He made his way to his bed and was soon dreaming:

Patriarch Dream I. A kindly but authoritative voice was speaking: "Herald, my son, wake up. Harken unto me for I have a mission."

Opening his eyes, my husband beheld a man with long,

white hair who was dressed in a flowing robe that belonged to a bygone day. The sandaled feet of this dignified personage did not touch the floor. They rested on a little cloud that floated beside the bed. The august visitor allowed my husband a moment of observation, then spoke again:

"Herald, my son, you have given your promise to a girl named Thelma. Now behold the eyes of a girl who lives in Denver, Colorado."

To his amazement, my husband had a sense of traveling through space and then found himself looking, soul-deep, into a pair of brown eyes he was never to forget.

Even before he was fully awake, my husband was at his closet door reaching for a suitcase on an upper shelf. He packed, feverishly, intent upon catching the next train that would take him from Boise, Idaho, to Denver, Colorado. But as he shut and strapped his suitcase, he was once more overcome by a drowsiness that compelled him back to his bed.

Patriarch Dream II. My husband heard a male voice calling his name. Upon opening his eyes, he beheld the patriarchal figure of his first dream, standing as before on a little cloud that floated about a foot off the floor. Once again, the ancient personage allowed a moment of observation and then spoke:

"My son, you are engaged to Thelma. Fulfill your promise and your time with her."

My husband woke up less inclined to rush off to Denver. He picked up his fiancée's picture, and as he studied it, he realized he was still in love. Within a few days, he regarded his desire to flee to Denver in search of an unknown woman as a dangerous impulse. Then came the day of his marriage rites in the great Salt Lake City Temple. In itself, this "sealing for time and all eternity" is simply an exchange of vows as the couple clasp hands across an altar and look into each other's eyes. But this ceremony has been preceded by a three-hour ritual in which people from all over the country don Biblical robes and join together in a dramatization of the Bible that proceeds from the creation in Genesis to the promises of heaven set forth in Revelations. This reinforcement of the fond teachings of his devout parents had a profound effect on my husband that can best be expressed in his own words: "I felt the hand of the Lord upon me. When it is my time to die, I shall turn my face toward the Temple."

Five years later, when my husband's first marriage failed in California, he lost more than a wife and the companionship of his son. The foundations of his faith were shaken. Often at night he walked the length of a long pier that extended out into the Pacific, fighting an urge to jump off and swim out beyond his endurance. Something always held him back, perhaps some dimly stirring memory of a dream that had hinted that all might yet be well. In an effort to forget the past, he worked furiously by day and, forsaking Mormon circles, engaged in the pleasures of the world by night. After a brief introduction to me in a restaurant, he met me again at a club party and asked me to dance. As we whirled out toward the center of the floor, our eyes locked and he smiled.

"I can tell you where you were living six years ago," he declared happily. "It was Denver, Colorado!"

Three months later, we were joined in a happy marriage that is now in its thirty-seventh year.

My husband's dreams of the patriarch were truly Great Dreams that evolved from the ESP levels of his subconscious to save his sanity and his life at a future date. They are all the more remarkable because my husband is not a psychic nor inclined toward mysticism. He can be classified as a non-dreamer, for he does not remember these productions, nor does he wish to take exercises that would make them more outstanding.

Although I classify the two patriarch dreams as Great Dreams in accord with the Jungian school of thought, I must admit that they did not spring from a totally virgin Jungian soil. The *wise old man* of my husband's dreams had been associatively prefigured for many years in my husband's mind. In the Mormon veneration of the Biblical patriarchs, these personages are regarded as actual forefathers of the faithful, and they are continually revived in Sunday School lessons and sermons in a personal Mormon connotation that depicts them as still active guardians of the church and its members. There is also a bit of Freudian psychology in these profound dreams, and two wishes are fulfilled. My husband admires women with brown eyes like those of his mother and his favorite sister, yet he had fallen in love with a grey-eyed woman. The two dreams allow him to have both.

But even as I make the above Freudian analysis of my husband's two Great Dreams, I am still romantic enough to be grateful that a strong emotional bond can be predestined and prefigured. It thrills me that life, like our dreams, is a strange interweaving of psychology and destiny.

I have had many turning points in my life, some of which, such as my interest in parapsychology, have affected the lives of others, even by the thousands. Yet in only one instance have I experienced a Great Dream. I think they are far more common in the lives of those given an extensive religious training in their early years than in cases like my own where religion played a small part during childhood. I also think these dreams are more apt to occur with the mystically inclined instead of to people as analytical as I. And I know for a fact that reading Jung produces more Jungian dreams than the norm. When a Jungian lecturer comes to town, I know that I shall be deluged by people reporting Jungian dreams and that even Great Dreams will be common, though in most of these instances, I think the Great Dreams are merely pseudo productions, triggered by lecture examples.

There are two categories of people who come to me for instruction: (1) those who have no outstanding psychic ability but wish to develop it; and (2) those who have a great deal of psychic ability and wish to channel it constructively. Mona

Mills, the brilliant young artist who authors Foster Art Books, is in the gifted category. When I first met Ms. Mills, others interested in parapsychology were so excited by her psychic potential that they wished to rush her into trance experiences. I, however, was of the opinion that it would be safer and more productive for her to begin training through my associative system of reading the tarot cards.

Characteristically, Ms. Mills made her decision psychically, through the following Great Dream.

The Tarot Card Dream. The dreamer, along with many other people, was walking along the edge of a curved promontory that edged a deep sea. All were naked because they wished to dive into the water. But first, they had to reach a building and apply for a ticket. Along the way, some fell into the sea, and others decided to dive in without tickets. None of these were seen again. When the dreamer reached the ticket building, a very pleasant young man gave her a smile of assurance, but instead of a ticket, he gave her a tarot card. Armed with this credential, she made the dive, surfaced easily, and swam safely to the lower shore of the promontory.

The main archetype in the *Tarot Card Dream* is the dreamer's animus, the young man who gives her a tarot card for a ticket. His pleasant demeanor indicates that the repressed masculine portion of her psyche is willing to cooperate in the tarot card venture. The sea in this dream is an archetypal representation of the unconscious whose depths must be dared during psychic pursuits. Although there is a Freudian wish fulfillment—the young man in the dream offering marriage (the ticket)—the total theme, from the Jungian perspective, is that my tarot system is a safe and effective method of psychic development. This dream guidance was totally correct. Ms. Mills developed safely and rapidly, for the archetypal tarot, when used associatively, is a natural path between unconscious and conscious processes. It also afforded a valuable frame of reference for Ms. Mills' astounding clairvoyant and medium-istic abilities.

Earlier in this chapter, I mentioned my one Great Dream. I shall recount it here because it is another dream that upholds Jung's theory of this particular phenomenon, a reality in the psychology of dreams that should not be lost to the world.

The Lapis Lazuli Dream. In the dream, I was dressed in a blue robe, a priestess of another time and place. I was totally fascinated by my work, the creation of a mandala with gemstones. The central stone was a huge lapis lazuli of deepest blue. I was embellishing the design with seed pearls that I placed around the stone, until I accomplished a complete circle.

The dream qualifies as great because it indicated an important turning point in my life and because it incorporates an archetype, the mandala. In the predictive sense, the blue of my robe and the blue of the stone represent psychic and spiritual interests, and the seed pearls are "gems of wisdom."

But the full predictive value of the dream was not revealed to me until two weeks had passed. At that time, a strange series of psychic events centering around a lapis lazuli—the deep blue gemstone to which the ancient Egyptians and Edgar Cayce attributed an inducement of psychic powers—was to plunge me into the research of geoplasmic and bioplasmic properties as they relate to psychic phenomena.

There is a profound inner meaning to the *Lapis Lazuli Dream*. Man, in endeavoring to find completion or the whole self, must not neglect his psychic faculties. He must develop them wisely and scientifically, yet with spiritual intent.

11

The ESP Content
of Classified Dreams

Psychologists and dream experts have discovered that certain dreams are so characteristic in the human experience that they can be set apart from the common dream and labeled to indicate their functioning or particular stimulus. Do these specializations rule out ESP content? In some cases, yes, and in other cases, no, as this chapter will inform you.

Here is the list of classifications that we shall examine for ESP possibilities:

1. Dreams of convenience
2. Anxiety dreams
3. Dreams caused by outer or inner stimuli
4. Mysophilic dreams
5. Typical dreams (dreams of menacing wild beasts, dreams of committing homicide, falling dreams, danger on mountain tops or ledges of buildings, flying dreams, dreams of being naked, dreams of missing boats or trains)

Dreams of Convenience

The dream of *convenience* is structured upon a wish fulfillment to relieve an actual biological necessity. These dreams attempt to *relieve hunger* by producing images of food or eating; or they attempt to *relieve thirst* by producing images of water and drinking. Or when there is a need to relieve the bladder, we dream of searching for a toilet, or the act of voiding. I have never found an ESP content in these dreams. However, dreams produced by the sexual urge, such as the emission dreams of men, seem to warn, sometimes, against an unfortunate sexual contact. But at the same time, these dreams are so psychological that their low incidence of relating to a coming event may be nothing more than pure chance.

Of course, we can dream sometimes of the biological urges when there is no pressing need for their relief, and on these occasions such dreams may have ESP possibilities, particularly if the mind has been trained toward this end or if there is a high quotient of native ESP. When I have an important deal pending that is not to go through, I usually dream that just as I am about to raise a brimming cup to my lips, an unseen hand dashes it to the floor, leaving me very chagrined about this "slip 'twixt the cup and lip." I am never conscious of thirst in these dreams, though it does seem desirable that I taste the contents of the cup.

The wish fulfillment in these dreams is hard to detect, for it has contradictory elements. But upon analysis, there can be little doubt that it harks back to my period of weaning. Although the cup is somewhat desirable, I hope it will be knocked to the floor so that I can again feed at the breast. The dream also reflects the chagrin I felt when I was a small child and fumbled my cup when trying to raise it to my lips.

Anxiety Dreams

As I have stated in a previous chapter, when dreams are

merely residues of worry, fear, or responsibility carried over from waking life, there is seldom an ESP content. Because there is no discernible wish fulfillment in anxiety dreams of this type, Jungians have a field day with them. They will select a dream of a person who has taken his worries to bed with him (dreams that Freud taught are lacking in latent wish fulfillment) and demand, "Now just where is the much-vaunted wish fulfillment theory to be found in this dream?" Of course, in these instances, the dreamer is wishing to find a way out of his problems by continuing to work on them at night.

But occasionally I have found a bit of wish fulfillment conducive to ESP in certain types of anxiety dreams that occur to many, yet they are identical in content to those dreams that do not contain ESP content. The *Examination Dream* is a case in point. Most of us have dreamed that we are back in school taking a final examination. Psychologists tell us we usually have these dreams when we are facing a critical situation in waking life. We revert to our school days because we have escaped the tensions attending that period, and we hope our fate will be the same in our present situation.

ESP is possible in these dreams through the insertion of another wish as was the case when, in the midst of an *Examination Dream*, the hand of an unseen person put a roll of twenty-dollar bills on my desk. Psychologically, money in a dream symbolizes love. Yes, I was much in love when I attended high school. Often I thought my romance was my only reward for having to attend. But in the perspective of ESP, the money indicated a reward for my efforts to solve the pressing problem in waking life that was causing me to dream.

Dreams Caused by Outer or Inner Stimuli

We have all experienced dreams caused or influenced by outer stimuli. It is commonplace for us to dream that our telephone is ringing and then to wake up to the fact that these sounds are taking place in the world of reality. On such occasions, we marvel at the way the dream incorporated this material into its structure as though knowing in advance that the sound was to occur—and this may very well be the case. Heretofore, the dream experts have theorized that the rapidity of the dream gives it ample time to incorporate sound effects. Others have held the opinion that these dreams are elaborated upon after we wake up. But the age of ESP has been ushered in at last, and we must not overlook the factor of prescience in subconscious processes. The following is an example that illustrates how the dream can convert an outer stimulus into an ESP production.

The Cold Breath Dream. I dreamed that I met a woman friend who pursed her lips and blew cold, repelling air into my face. I awoke suddenly, very uncomfortable because the wind had blown open a French window at the head of my bed and cold air was actually blowing on my face. A short time later, the friend of whom I had dreamed treated me in a very cold and arrogant manner at a time when I most needed her help and encouragement.

Experience has taught me that the *conversion of physical stimuli to psi perception* is basic to ESP in general. A student of mine reports that she has many psi experiences with objects seen along the road as she drives. At one time, as she approached a piece of discarded wrapping paper, it looked like a huge check; but as she came closer, she saw this piece of refuse in its true perspective. When she reached home and picked up her mail, she discovered a large book royalty check that she had not expected at that time. On another occasion, she thought she saw a sick dog lying in the road, and she was relieved when she realized she had not seen a dog but only an old tire. However, that night, a friend tearfully told her that her dog had been poisoned.

In his *Structure and Dynamics of the Psyche,* Jung remarks that it "frequently happens" that one mistakes a stranger on the street for an old friend, a disappointment that is assuaged by running into this old friend—who may just have returned from a distance—on the next corner.

Exercises to be given in a forthcoming chapter will have a relationship to the conversion of physical stimuli to psi perception, for I shall teach you how to store impressions of the physical senses in the preconscious so that your ESP faculty can utilize them in both the night dream and in clairvoyance during waking hours.

Inner Stimuli Dreams

Conditions of the body often stimulate dreams. A woman who dreamed that an eagle was clawing her shoulder woke up to the pain of bursitis. When the dream faculty is trained, inner stimuli can produce meaningful connotations in most ingenious ways. At one time I had to have a small growth removed from my left breast. Naturally, my family and I were apprehensive as we waited for the biopsy report that would indicate whether or not this growth was cancerous. That night I dreamed I had a stopped up nose. The symptom frightened me so much that I picked up the telephone and demanded that our family physician leave his bed, in the dead of night, and come at once. He arrived, examined my nose, and gave me a sound scolding: "Why did you get me out of bed for so small a matter as this? Don't you know it's just a head cold? I assure you your worry over this small malady is foolish."

I awakened to the fact that I had developed a head cold, but I was happy. I knew the laboratory report would be a blessed negative. It was.

Mysophilic Dreams

The anatomy of the human body is well established. We know we have organs such as the heart, liver, and lungs that have an autonomous functioning that needs no conscious guidance. We also know that the unseen portions of the body sometimes fall subject to diseases that pursue autonomous courses. Often when we fall ill, we do not know what ails us until we consult a diagnostician—and then we are often surprised. For example, a friend of mine was told, recently, that there was nothing wrong with the big toe that was giving her excruciating pain. The condition denoted disease in another area, a uremic acid imbalance.

We have the same problem with the subconscious mind. There are sections of the inner psyche of which the lay person has no knowledge. These sections function autonomously, as do their diseases. This is why there is often a reaction to a psychiatrist's diagnosis such as the following imaginary example: "No, Doctor, I don't hate my father. As I keep trying to tell you, I am here because I have a history of attacking my employers." But aren't employers "father figures"?

If we could actually see the mechanism of the subconscious and its parts, we would discover atavistic, animalistic, and race memory vestiges such as castration fears, cannibalism, sadism, and mysophilic tendencies (a lustful attitude toward dirt, excretions, etc.), and we would learn that these abominations that have been buried beneath years of conscious progress still haunt the subconscious and form their own constellations of conscious influence.

Freud knew that the anal sadistic stage through which infants pass is often attended by a pronounced interest in defecation and its products. Even Jung agreed that this fascination for the waste products of the body is a normal stage of infant development. In some mental aberrations, patients actually regress to this stage. Because of the mysophylic and anal sadistic residues in the human subconscious, psychologists are not surprised that these tendencies sometimes surface in our dreams. It must be remembered that we all "go crazy" when we dream.

We have the recorded history of fastidious people who dream that mischievous children or imps are spreading feces all over themselves and the house. The children and imps in these dreams are, of course, the dreamer himself acting under the compulsion of a regressive wish fulfillment that would be intolerable in waking life.

Recurring dreams of urine, feces, and other filth, in proportion to other dream material, indicate that these dreams are purely psychological, containing no ESP content. If such dreams occur with the same characters, locale, etc., they are doubly suspect.

But the occasional dream of feces has a psychological symbolism that can also be predictive—*money*!

The first work of the infant is to make abdominal and anal contractions, a "job" that brings him the relief of expelled feces. This is why the nonrecurring feces dream often predicts money that is to be made or earned, not found or received as a gift. For example, a student who sells vitamins dreamed that she went to the bathroom and produced a large, blue feces (blue is coded to mean healing). A short time later, she began to sell a laxative that had a good markup and that proved to be a top repeat sales item.

Another student, who made her living in a business in which she dealt with a class of people who were beneath her financially and socially, dreamed that she was sent to appraise a slum dwelling. She was shocked that the tenants of one apartment had defecated everywhere, even in their dishes. My interpretation of this dream was that my student would soon be making a great deal more money. I was correct.

Dreams of urine often predict illness, or the need for a physical checkup. Foul odors from feces, urine, or bowel gas often predict scandal or false accusations made by others. Sometimes foul odors for which we can find no apparent cause are experienced in dreams. We have all heard the slang expression that someone is "raising a big stink" about a trivial or unintended offense.

Typical Dreams

In the designations made by dream experts, those dreams

that occur most frequently are classified as *typical*. The typical dreams that we shall now examine for ESP content are: dreams of being threatened or attacked by wild animals; dreams of homicide; dreams of falling; dreams of danger on mountain tops or ledges of tall buildings; dreams of flying; dreams of being naked or inadequately clothed; and dreams of missing boats or trains.

Dreams of Being Threatened or Attacked by Wild Animals

Some moralistic dream interpreters hold that dreams in which wild beasts appear are warnings that we must exert control over our tempers lest we harm others. Because the human subconscious will follow a provided code, when it is trained to do so, this interpretation may be true in some instances—but never in those dreams in which wild beasts menace us to the point of terror or actual attack, causing suffering. Psychologists know that menacing or attacking dream beasts represent *repressed animosity* that is seldom unleashed in waking life. Many who suffer such nightmares are actually lacking in proper anger responses.

The roots of these dreams usually date back to the anal sadistic stage in childhood. The wild beast that threatens or inflicts wounds is, according to my findings, a parent who was overly punitive, too easily chagrined into corporal punishment, during the phase of life when the infant is rebellious, negative, and prone to autoeroticism and temper tantrums. When a child is given corporal punishment before he is old enough to understand that correction is for his own good, he is in a psychological double bind. Instinctively, he wants to fight back, but when he does so, he is attacking his source of security and love. When the child's animosity is repressed, it often surfaces in dreams in which the wish to attack is inverted in a punishment that he receives himself.

In my files I have several case histories in which people dreamed, as children, that they had two mothers, one good and the other bad and unpredictable. One example of such a recurring dream is tragic—a little girl who dreamed that she had ten or twelve mothers. In the dream they sat in a circle, each beautifully dressed and sweet, as the child stood in the center and tried to choose her real parent. Each "mother" held out her arms invitingly, declaring that she was the real mother and imploring the child to come to her. But the little girl who so longed to find her mother had to be extremely careful. If she made the wrong choice, as she invariably did, the mother to whom she went would turn into a bear and claw her until it drew blood. At the time I investigated this case, the dreamer was a grown woman. She recalled that her mother had been either extremely lenient and affectionate or so abusive in correction that neighbors objected. Actions that elicited smiles of indulgence on one day would call for the whip the next. The recurring dream was a diagnostic prognostication, for the wild beast in the mother was scarring the child for life, making her masochistic.

Jung believed that dreams of menacing or attacking wild beasts denote a dangerous sex repression. This is likely to be the case when horses are the dream animals, for horses often represent the sex drive.

I do not go along with dream interpreters who state that animals in our dreams represent our "animal nature." Certainly this is seldom the case when dreams have been directed toward producing feats of ESP.

Dreams of Homicide

Helen Keller, the amazing woman who learned how to converse, read, and write after scarlet fever had stricken her blind and deaf at the age of eighteen months, was still able to dream, though not in the audio or visual sense. When men of science queried Helen Keller about her dreams, she revealed that she was quite capable of homicide during her nocturnal adventures, never hesitating to kill anyone who dared attack one she loved. However, she often heaped verbal abuse upon these same loved ones, chastising and belittling them unmercifully, and she complained that these dreams became more frequent and abusive as she grew older. These dreams date back to the hostility of the anal sadistic stage in which Miss Keller's rages had been compounded by the frustration of noncommunication, The wish to attack a loved one is cleverly handled by the dream censor who makes a substitution, which is not the case in her dreams of verbal abuse.

The dreams grew worse as Helen grew older for a very good reason: Helen's parents decided that she was never to have suitors. They were afraid some man would wish to marry this remarkable woman in order to exhibit her talents for money. Helen's loss of womanly fulfillment was poignantly portrayed in her dreams. In a recurring episode, she "climbed and climbed," enduring this torture in her "passionate desire," as she described it, "to find an object to hold on to" (a husband).

In another dream account, Helen found herself tossing restlessly upon her bed. She decided that she must rise and read a certain book. The book she desired had no name, but she always found it easily on the shelf upon which it was kept in her dream house. She sat down, placed the book upon her knee, and lovingly pored over a page. Alas, it was a complete blank, as she somehow knew it must be. Her tears began to fall, and she closed the book lest they mar a message that was not there.

The book represents the *book of life*, and Helen sought a page that was never to be written. In the Freudian fixed symbology, a book has a female connotation, and the blank page denotes Helen's unfulfillment as a wife and mother.

Dreams of Falling

These dreams date back to the infant's innate, unlearned fear of falling and are perhaps atavistic, harking still further back to the danger of falling from one of man's first homes, the tree. Freudian psychologists claim that falling dreams indicate a desire to fall from grace. It is interesting to note that Helen Keller's climbing dreams often ended in a fall, "downward and still downward" until she dissolved into the atmosphere.

Dreams of Danger on Mountain Tops or Ledges of Tall Buildings

These dreams, like Helen Keller's dangerous climbing, represent both the fear and the attraction of a temptation.

Dreams of Flying

In Chapter 6, I discussed the psychological aspects and the limited coding possibilities for these experiences. Here I wish to discuss their associative perspective, which affords a great deal more leeway for paranormal expression.

For some reason or other—possibly because I had no burning conscious desire—neither my cards nor my dreams ever predicted a degree of international fame for me. On my fifty-second birthday, nothing was further from my mind than the achievement of recognition on a worldwide scale. But a dear old Spiritualist friend, Rev. Herbert Skelton, came to spend the day with me, and as we sipped coffee after dinner, the Reverend read for members of my family. When he came to me he paused for some time, then spoke:

"You are going to gain the attention of the world in some spectacular way. Later, you will write a book on dreams that will make you a famous woman."

Rev. Skelton had always given remarkably accurate readings, but this time I smiled. I knew I had a great deal to give to the world concerning ESP, but I thought that all I had to do was to inform top parapsychologists of my findings and that these scientists would then test and perfect my methods and give them to the world in their own names. I doubt that my letters got past the secretaries of some of the scientists to whom I wrote. Finally, I realized that all the work of relating my findings to the known sciences, and all the work of reaching the public, was strictly up to me. But how was I to reach the public?

Then one day I received the first glimmering of an international prediction in my cards, an incident concerning a ship at sea that came to pass before the day was over. To test the possibility of making national predictions further, I programmed the first Clay-Liston fight into my deck of coded cards and then shuffled and laid them out for study. Clay appeared with cards of success and victory; Liston with cards of chagrin and defeat. There was also an interesting touch that lifted the prediction out of the fifty-fifty category of chance averages—an indication that Liston would claim a doublecross.

When this prediction came to pass, I remembered Rev. Skelton's prophecy. Was the door toward the recognition of my applied ESP sciences opening? Was I to call attention to my claims by making and publishing national and international predictions? Was this what God wanted of me? I fell asleep wondering, and that night I received my answer in the following dream.

The Flying in School Dream. I was back in the eighth grade in school, giggling and passing notes as had been my habit. Then I noticed that the teacher and my classmates were looking at me with a strange silent supplication. "OK," I said, "I'll show you it can be done." Leaving my desk, I went up to the front of the room where I stood poised, for a few seconds, with my arms outstretched like wings. Then I spoke. "Now look all you kids. I can fly! I can fly! I can fly!" Yes, I could! The rest of the class must have thought they were dreaming.

Putting facetiousness aside, the psychology of the above dream differs from the Freudian sex thrill flying dreams. It must be classified in accord with Adler's "psychology of the ego," for it is a dream of powers above the norm. The dream inspired me to make and publish the national and international predictions that have been essential to the sale of the books and courses that present my breakthrough methodologies.

Dreams of Being Naked or Inadequately Clothed

Most of us have dreamed of being naked or only partially clothed in the presence of others. These dreams hark back to the childhood wish of ridding ourselves of our clothes, and, psychologically, they indicate a subconscious exhibitionism that the censor punishes by making us feel so embarrassed that we try to hide.

At one time I thought that dreams of nakedness, especially if accompanied by embarrassment, could be of no ESP value. But the following dream, with its symbolism so exquisitely meaningful to a coming event, changed my mind.

The Pink Slip Dream. Dressed only in my slip, I stood on a raised platform in the center of my neighborhood shopping mall while thousands of shoppers swirled around me. I tried to get off the platform so that I could escape the public eye, but I could not.

When I awoke from this dream, I realized that it had not been nebulous but was as substantial as many of my dreams that have precognitive value. Also, I had two symbols. A mistake is often referred to as a *slip*, and the *public platform* and the thousands of people indicated the mistake would be publicized. Armed with these clues, I guessed what the "slip" would be. I had had a successful two-year association with the *National Enquirer*. I can say to their credit that, when I approached them for publicity concerning the direct hits I had made in foretelling events in Senator Edward Kennedy's life, they made a thorough check with the Western Union Telegraph Company. To their amazement, they learned that I had documented eight direct hits, including a warning that I saw "death signs" around the senator just two days before the night-black waters of Chappaquiddick Bay closed over the top of his car. The senator won his battle against death, but his pretty companion, Mary Jo Kopechne, did not. After that, I submitted other predictions to the *Enquirer*, one of them that the grand jury would acquit the senator of wrongdoing in this tragedy.

But on one occasion, the *Enquirer* quoted me incorrectly, possibly because I had been queried over the telephone. Blaring forth in front page headlines, they told the world that I had predicted Senator Kennedy would lose his Senate seat in the forthcoming election. In talking with their reporter, my exact words had been: "I am puzzled about contradictory signs that appear in my cards when I process Senator Kennedy's campaign. I shall be surprised if he wins this election. He will either lose or the election will be attended by a misfortune or a loss of some kind." The senator did not lose the election, he won. Nevertheless, his victory was dampened when some of his most trusted colleagues reacted to the Chappaquiddick incident by divesting him of his position as the Senate's Democratic Whip.

So there I was—standing in my "slip" before fifty thousand readers! I am now convinced that the dream was predictive, for I have since had other "slip" dreams that related to a coming embarrassment.

Dreams of Missing Boats or Trains

When family members go off on dream boats and trains that we are unable to catch, most psychologists believe we are fulfilling a wish that they die before we do. But when we miss a boat or a train that does not carry away our family, we are in a state of anxiety about an ambition or goal we fear we shall not be able to accomplish.

My final word on typical dreams is that their resolution can be predictive. Consider it a good omen if you are rescued from that dangerous mountain top or building ledge, as well as if you finally manage to catch the boat or train that has so often eluded you. And if you win in dreams of combat, as Helen Keller so often did, you are apt to have the courage and determination that will make you a winner in the game of life.

12

Psychic Exercises for ESP Dreams

The information contained in this chapter often develops both the dream faculty and general ESP powers. Physiologists and psychologists now know that everyone dreams, but, unfortunately, there are some who can't recall their dreams the next day. I have solved this problem for many of my students by enabling them to dream more vividly, and in some instances the stuff of dreams becomes so objective that guidance symbols are glimpsed, for a few seconds, even during hours when the student is wide awake, perhaps while performing a daily task or engaged in conversation with another. But psychic development is an individual process, and in a few instances, objectified waking hour symbols were reported by students who still could not remember their dreams—perhaps because they slept too soundly, or because the censor did not want the psychological content to reach the level of conscious appraisal. Even those students who noticed no dream acceleration, either by night or by day, often reported a noticeable increase of intuitive guidance hunches.

It goes without saying that a colorful dream is more vivid, and therefore more likely to be remembered, than a gray or black and white production. And when we dream in color, we have a valuable tool, for colors can be coded according to the following table:

Red: Danger
Blue: Friendly, harmless, benign, spiritual
Brown: Business
Rose or pink: Good health, well being
Purple: Ability, prestige, power
Orange: Rivalry, contention
Black: Trouble, sorrow
Green: Life, new interests, money
White: Favorable, pure, innocent—a "yes" answer to questions
Yellow: Multiplies the good aspects of a dream and promises a solution for any present or future problem that the dream may reveal

The general exception to the above table is that when objects appear in their normal color the code does not apply. For instance, because tomatoes are naturally red, red tomatoes do not signify danger in a dream.

Always note the color of the clothing worn by yourself and other dream characters. Although brown is the "business" color, brown clothing often denotes illness. However, clothes that are of good material and cut are always a good omen. A person who appears in a dream in well-fitting brown clothing will recover from an illness. Well-fitting black clothes indicate dignity instead of trouble or sorrow.

Skin tones in a dream also deviate from the above table in some instances. A person with a red face is embarrassed, and a person with red hands is likely to be "caught red-handed" in some misconduct. He is not in danger unless he is dressed in red. Green skin tones indicate envy and jealousy. Yellow skin tones denote cowardice; saffron skin tones, liver trouble.

Experience has taught me that, in many cases, color consciousness in dreams can be acquired through the exercises presented in this chapter. Over sixty years ago, Professor William S. Morrow of the State Normal School of Westfield, Massachusetts, attempted to measure the effect of colored objects on dreams. He instructed twenty pupils in his psychology class to stare intently, from two to ten minutes before going to bed, at paper cutouts arranged in the following sequence: a green square; a violet octagon; a red square; a violet heart; a green robin; a yellow coffee cup; a blue maltese cross; a pink circle; a blue triangle; a green hen; and a blue hen. The next morning the students reported forty-seven dreams, all of which were in color. But in the interest of dreaming true, it is best not to associate objects with color as Professor Morrow did. Instead, use the number one exercise given in the following list.

Color Exercises

1. Cut squares from vividly colored paper or cloth. Concentrate intently on these colors from five to ten minutes before going to bed.

2. Become more color conscious during the day, noting well the shadings of the colors that surround you.

3. Here is a dynamic color exercise. Sit with an empty glass placed three feet away from you on an otherwise clear table. Look at the glass intently and imagine how it would look if filled with blue liquid. After a minute or two, progress from blue to green liquid—then to red, yellow, purple, and orange. As you become sensitive, you may note a response within yourself to each color change. For instance, the progression from green to red may match the faint sensation that is felt after striking middle C on the piano keyboard and then progressing to the next tone above, D. Change the order of the colors frequently.

4. Choose a color and imagine that all your carpets, drapes, linens, clothing, etc., are in this one hue. Do this

several times a day for two days. On the third day choose another color and work with it for two days. Proceed until you have exercised with all the colors.

5.   If it is difficult for you to imagine colors in the above exercises, work with the squares you have cut out from paper or cloth for the first exercise. Look at a color until it is firmly in mind, then look away from the color and endeavor to recall it mentally.

6.   After you have developed a good color consciousness, choose a color, let us say red, then mentally "see" all the shades of this color that you can recall—cerise, vermillion, rose, pink, etc. The next day, do the same exercise with another color. Continue this exercise until you can mentally recall the various shades of each color easily.

Even those who are able to dream in color should take the above exercises for a few weeks, for color awareness has a direct relationship to ESP.

Concentration Exercises

The above exercises require a degree of concentration, and the ability to concentrate consciously is so helpful to subconscious ESP processes that most yoga systems present exercises to strengthen this type of thought. Unfortunately, these yoga exercises require so much concentration in their own context that they are often difficult for the person who thinks he can't maintain an intense attention span on any one thought or object. Fortunately, man has a great aid for concentration, the pencil, which allows him to jot down facts and keep them in mind as he presses on toward other objectives necessary to an integrated thought pattern. For this reason, I always give my students written exercises in order to develop their concentration.

For example, as I write, I am looking at a picture with which I have trained many students. First, I have them take a brief glance at the picture as a whole—a charming scene that leads the gaze through the hallway of a lovely home and out through the front door to a path flanked with flower gardens. This path leads to an iron gate, and beyond the gate, across the street, is a large dwelling set among trees.

After my student has observed this picture for a few seconds, I seat him at a table from which he can see the picture and give him a pencil and paper, asking him to list all the objects he can see, beginning with the foreground of the picture, the floor of the hallway. Usually, the student manages a written report such as the following: The floor is hardwood with a small rug that does not run the entire length of the hall. There is a grandfather clock against the left wall that juts into the hallway; it is flanked with pictures on both sides. A table sits next to the right wall of the hall. Upon this table is a vase of flowers, and above this table are two pictures. A chandelier is affixed to the ceiling. The front door of the hall is open, and there is a path that leads to an iron gate. There is a house across the street.

When the student signifies that he has finished this exercise, I tell him I want him to perform it again, this time giving me as many added details as possible about each item he has listed. This second report usually reveals that the hardwood floor is highly polished and that the rug is of a blue and white mottled material with a white fringe. The base of the grandfather clock is broad and plain, but the long center portion leading to the face is inlaid with carving, and the carved ornamentation that crowns the top is in three sections. And so my student continues until he has added details to every item he has listed previously. Furthermore, the student often finds objects in the picture that he has missed before, such as a vase upon the table.

I conclude this concentration exercise by requesting my student to look closely for any details he may have missed on his second list. Much to his surprise, the student usually finds that he missed several interesting features of the picture while making up his first two lists—it may be that he discovers that the hands of the grandfather clock indicate that it is eleven, that there is a mat before the door, that the door is blue, a fact that he missed before, and so on until the entire picture has been reviewed for the third time.

With practice, my students are able to attain a power of concentration that allows them to look at a picture for a moment or two and then look away and recall it in their mind's eye in remarkable detail.

Exercises in Perception

The exercises in perception to be presented here are not a new concept, for their origins date back to word of mouth instructions from India to Egypt. Later, they were printed as "secret lessons" by various occult societies. And finally, psychic researchers of the caliber of Hereward Carrington found them efficacious for developing clairvoyant and clair-audient abilities. However, I give valuable added information in most of the areas that this work covers. For instance, many teachers will tell you to exercise for "psychic vision" by imagining that you are holding a rose in your hand, "seeing" it as clearly as possible. While this exercise is good, so far as it goes, many areas of perception can be added. Don't just "see" the imagined rose. Get a firm sense of the stem being held between the thumb and forefinger of your left hand while you explore its leaves and feel gingerly for thorns with your right hand. Lift the rose to your nostrils and "inhale" its fragrance. Brush its lovely petals against your cheek.

Another exercise popular in ESP classes is the visualization of a dove perched on the right forefinger. But again, I teach a more total perception. Hold out your right forefinger and mentally "see" the dove flying toward you. "Hear" the flap of the dove's wings as its tiny claws curl around your finger. Note how it rocks back and forth for balance and cocks its head toward your face. When it flies away, "hear" the wing motion and add another imaginary sensation—the faint odor of musty dust that is fanned up into your face.

Occultists have long theorized that man has a spiritual counterpart of the physical body in which all the organs and faculties are duplicated. It is their belief that exercises in imaginary perception strengthen our "spiritual" or "astral" eyes, ears, olfactory senses, etc., for clairvoyant-clairaudient purposes. While I do not dismiss the theory of a spiritual body, I know that from the standpoint of psychology we must theorize that exercises in perceptual imagination strengthen the memory of these sensations in the preconscious, allowing it an input from which it can feed back psi experiences and more vivid and dimensional dreams.

Exercises for Oral and Olfactory Psychic Effects

Exercises that rely upon the imagination to imitate the oral and olfactory senses are highly conducive to the reception of ESP. Some of the better psychics whom I have researched rely upon oral perceptions to an amazing degree. Six or seven years ago, San Diego psychic Oliver Force asked me to test his ability. I arranged an interview in my own home, and as Mr. Force seated himself in one of my living room chairs, he asked me to go into my own room, fill a box with small items, and then hold the box three feet away from him while he endeavored to name the objects. Instead of following these directions, I went to a storage chest in the den and picked up a small box of polished gemstones in order to make Mr. Force's test far more difficult than the perception of items off a dresser such as perfume bottles and combs that might be arrived at by guess. Without allowing Mr. Force to handle the box, I held it three feet away from him as he had directed. Mr. Force began to make motions with his mouth and his tongue. "I am tasting items that are round, hard, and polished," he stated. "Are there gemstones in the box?" I nodded my head in astonishment, and Mr. Force volunteered further information, telling me that two of the gemstones had been made into jewelry. I thought he was wrong, but when I opened the box, I discovered that my husband had placed a cufflink and a necklace pendant in the box without my knowledge.

Cultivating an imaginary sense of taste is simple. Scan your refrigerator, cupboard, and medicine chest, then seat yourself in a comfortable position and imagine yourself tasting the various items one at a time. Get a full taste sensation. For instance, sugar is not merely sweet, it is also granular and quick-dissolving. Castor oil coats the tongue and produces gagging.

Take the above exercise once or twice a day for fifteen minute intervals. After three days, switch to olfactory sensations for a time, ranging from perfume to vinegar, from chemicals to floral scents, over a wide range of possible sensations.

Exercises for Psychic Tactile Sensations

Exercise for tactile impressions by setting out an array of small items such as pencils, combs, erasers, rings, etc. Handle each item and set it down again. Next time around, handle each item with your eyes closed. During the third session, handle each item again, with the eyes closed. As soon as you set it down, hold your hands over the item while you endeavor to recapture the sensations you felt when you handled it.

Another important exercise is to imagine that you are handling textures—silk, wool, linen, fur, canvas, foil, sandpaper, etc.

Picture Exercises

Find a picture of a group of men and women in a scene that stirs the imagination. I have an inexpensive print of an eighteenth century French court scene that I use for two purposes: (1) exercises that upgrade ESP perception in general, including dreams; (2) a specific exercise for making dream productions realistic and dimensional. In this picture, six women, gowned in the full-skirted silk and satin elegance of a bygone day, and six white-wigged men are enjoying a concert of chamber music. Three of the group are musicians, and one is a young woman who has risen from her chair to sing.

I begin my exercises by gaining a sense of movement accompanied by sound. Even those who are paying attention to the music are fidgeting a bit in their seats. Two of the women aren't even pretending to listen. Mentally, I "hear" them giggle as they lift fans and kerchiefs to their faces to hide the merriment derived from their titillating gossip. The singer changes her stance, occasionally, and looks briefly at the sheet of music in her hands. The enraptured violinist sways a bit, and the pianist glances away from her nimble fingers and smiles as they complete a difficult run.

Next, I choose a character, the singer for instance, and become completely acquainted with her. I pass the textures of her silks, satins, and velvet ribbons between my fingers; I "listen" to her voice; and I feel the rounded flesh of her arm as I circle my fingers around it. Finally, I imagine that I am this singer. The next day I choose a different character, perhaps the sensitive violinist or the jolly appearing cellist, and become him!

In an exercise that is a specific for dreaming, I hang the picture on the wall opposite my bed. I get a sense of movement and sound from the picture and then look at it without training my concentration on any one aspect until it is time to turn off the light. I then visualize the picture in life-size dimensions and "step into" it, sometimes as one of the characters and at other times as a newcomer, dressed in the fashion of the other ladies. As I doze off, I am sometimes actually dreaming of the picture. Even if I don't have this dream experience, I know the exercise has been good, for it never fails to boost dream power after a fallow period.

But do not overdo this exercise with any one picture or it will cease to be effective. I have another picture, one of robed figures ascending and descending the stairs leading to a temple, that gives my subconscious a renewed interest after I have become tired of the first picture.

Dream Words that Lead and Guide

The spoken word has been especially valuable in my dreams—not just as a play upon words, but often as direct and forthright as a conversation in daily life. Friends and relatives, both the living and the dead, are often very wise when I meet them in the dream world. Quite obligingly— usually at the end of a dream—they impart good advice, predict the future, or answer a pressing question. And sometimes a living friend or a relative tells me something he needs to know for himself. The next day I contact this person and pass along the information.

Begin exercises for vocal auditory impressions by seating yourself in a comfortable position. The words *yes* and *no* are the most important with which to work, for often a dream figure will point to an object and say "yes" or "no." For instance, at a time when you are wondering whether or not to move, a dream figure may point to a trunk and say "NO!" Begin by imagining that you hear the word *yes* reverberating around you, first faintly, then more and more distinctly until the impression becomes boldly loud. On the second day, work with the word *no* in the same way. On the third day, repeat the exercise with the word *yes*, then reinforce the impression by imagining a hand writing the word *yes* on a blackboard every time the word is spoken. Take the same exercise with the word *no* on the next day.

On another day, make a list of your friends and relatives. Imagine that each one comes up to you in turn and says "yes" in his own vocal inflection and tone. Do the same exercises with the word *no*.

Recall the voices of movie and television stars. Try to imitate them. Read a sentence from a book, then imagine that you hear a voice reciting this sentence.

Vocal Chord Exercises

Because dream experts have discovered that there is often movement in the vocal chords during our nocturnal productions, I give my students exercises in "silent speaking." Begin by saying your own name and the names of your family and friends in your normal tone of voice. Next, whisper this list of names. Continue by saying the words inaudibly, but with full lip movement. Finally, repeat the names with no lip movement, depending entirely upon your vocal chords.

Repeat the above exercises with advisory phrases such as the following:

You are right.
Take it easy.
Don't be lazy.
Hold your fire.
You win.
Get to work.
Use tact.
Forget it.
Check your car.
Don't be greedy.
No hurry.
Mind your own business.
Live and let live.
Get a physical checkup.
Don't make important changes
   now.
Go ahead, take a chance.
Haste makes waste.
Right a wrong.
Avoid this person.
Something better is coming.
You are making a mistake.

Don't give up.
Be kind and gentle.
Watch expenditures.
Snap it up, time is of the
   essence.
Watch your temper.
Let sleeping dogs lie.
Don't become emotionally
   involved.
Watch out, beware!
Trust your own judgment.
Stop it.
Follow through with your plans.
Get your rest.
Don't go too far.
Make a fresh start.
Another needs your love and
   encouragement.
No need to fear.
Take the advice of another.
Keep your own counsel.
Guard secrets.

Revenge will backfire.

Honesty is the best policy.

Don't be too trusting.

Wait a while.

Don't decide now.

Wait for further developments.

Get away, flee.

Don't be rash.

Quit wasting your time.

Shoulder your responsibilities.

Check into this.

Proceed, but with caution.

Shame on you!

As I have stated before, the person who has trained his dream faculty no longer needs to examine each dream character in accord with the Jungian theory that he will discover his own faults in the dream depiction of others. When I am decidedly in the wrong and trying to rationalize, some dream character, usually my stepfather, sets me straight; I believe that I am indebted to exercises taken with the above list of phrases for this moral guidance. This arrangement with my superego frees my dream characters to represent their own virtues and follies in accord with the ESP content of the dream.

Of course, we are the creators of our own dream characters, except in rare instances when telepathic factors may be involved. And when our dream characters speak to us, it is our vocal muscles that move to pronounce their words. This is fortunate, for our hunch power can often "speak" to us by manipulating our vocal chords during the day. I do not experience exteriorized voice in the same way that I experience exteriorized objectified visual symbols. But I do sometimes hear an inner voice—a sensation that seems to travel from the solar plexus region to my throat at the same time that I get a strong impression of word-formed guidance. For instance, I once thought I would have to start court proceedings in order to collect some money that was due me. But when I picked up the telephone to contact a lawyer, my inner voice sent a strong, almost verbal, message—"Hold your fire!" Soon the party who owed the money offered to make small but regular payments. I was happy to accept, for I do not like to inconvenience and pressure others when it can be avoided.

A Success Secret

I have discovered that the exercises given in this chapter are much more effective when they are reinforced by programming. Just before taking an exercise, and at intervals during the exercise if it is a long session, point to your solar plexus area and make firm declarations such as the following:

1. My subconscious is awake and alert to this exercise.
2. I am now opening a channel for input and feedback between conscious and subconscious ESP processes.
3. My subconscious will use the input of sensations in this exercise to feed back meaningful dreams and hunches.

Programming is so essential to my methodology of ESP dreaming that the next two chapters will be devoted to its dynamic potential and specialized applications.

13

Advanced
Programming Techniques

This chapter is designed to give the reader a remarkable control over his dreams. Heretofore in this book I have dealt with *spontaneous dream guidance*. Now I shall reveal the secrets of programming the subconscious during the day so that it will give *specific dream guidance* or answer a specific question. I shall also teach suggestions that train the mind to use dream books, if this seems necessary, and I shall present dynamic direct and indirect suggestion-programming techniques.

Programming is a word that we usually associate with computers—those marvelous arithmetical and analogical machines that work with such uncanny speed that they seem to shrink time as they provide answers, within minutes, when it would take a human mind hours or days to work out the same problem—a situation that has led us to believe, erroneously, that our "thinking machines" are superior to the human mind.

But we have not reckoned with the subconscious. It is the superior computer. Within the brief span of a dream, or during the few seconds it takes to shuffle a deck of coded cards, it can bridge both time and space. Computers are provided with limited memory banks through which they can sort and sift to provide answers. But the preconscious has a store of personal memories, and the unconscious, in the collective sense, has a vast memory bank as old as time from which the ESP faculty can discern analogies and reach conclusions concerning points of time and space that cannot be arrived at through conscious mental processes.

When we use computers, we often program their memory banks toward the processing of specific data. We can use this same technique with our dreams. In fact, this book already has presented a valuable programming technique—the arbitrary coding found in popular dream books. It may seem superfluous to supplement nature's great data bank, the personal and the collective unconscious, with a code; but through analysis and experience, we learn two facts: (1) without the aid of a code, the ESP determinant in dreams is mainly restricted to association; it cannot give a total performance; and (2) the ESP determinant is able and usually eager to use a provided code that can upgrade its performance. As I pointed out in *The Cybernetic ESP Breakthrough*, subconscious processes are highly analogous to conscious processes. The conscious mind needs tools such as books, pencils, diagrams, etc., for its training and expression; the subconscious needs card codes, crystal balls, and popular dream books.

I have improved the ability of even great psychics by introducing them to a coded frame of reference they can use in conjunction with their telepathic, psychometric, and associative powers. But some psychics with little talent feel that an arbitrary code is an affront to their limited ability. Such people sell their ESP faculties short. When the subconscious expresses a message via a code, it is performing a feat fully as great as surfacing a message through associative processes.

One great advantage of using a coded methodology in dreams is that we can code *yes* and *no* symbols. When this technique is mastered, a *white object* in a dream denotes an *affirmative* or cheerful answer to a specific question, whereas a *black object* tells us *no* or gives an unhappy prognosis.

Begin training your subconscious to this technique in the following manner. For several days, point to your solar plexus area as you turn your attention inward and "talk" to your subconscious mind as though it were an entity separate from yourself. Impress this "inner-self" by telling it for several days that it is becoming capable of answering your questions through the presentation of either a black or a white dream symbol whenever you shall demand such a signal. Deliberately point out white and black objects as though instructing a child. Keep reminding the subconscious that white is fortunate and a *yes* signal and that black is a warning or a *no* signal. After several days of this exercise, you will be ready to make an actual experiment.

During the day, write out a question on a piece of paper. I use a half sheet of typing paper. Whenever you think of your question, reread it and "tell" your subconscious mind that it will answer correctly during the night by presenting either a white or a black symbol and that you will remember this symbol when you wake up the next morning.

When you retire, hold the question to your forehead at a point between your eyes and declare: "If the answer to this question is *yes*, I shall dream of white. If the answer to this question is *no*, I shall dream of black." Slip the paper beneath your pillow, or beneath the sheet under your head if you do not use a pillow.

If you do not dream of a black or a white object the first night, repeat the process until you do. Sometimes an entire dream will be white, or black, such as a landscape covered with snow or soot. At other times the signal object may be very small. In either event, the question has been answered. If this answer proves to be correct thank the inner self, or the subconscious mind, for obeying orders. Praise it for its remarkable ability.

I am not the originator of the black and white dream method. It is very old—as old as Egypt. But the ancients who first used this method implanted the suggestion by beseeching an angel to send the correct signal. Nothing was known about cybernetics, computers, programming, or the subconscious mind. From Egypt, the method found its way into the secret occult societies of Europe. When I discovered it, during my research, I upgraded it with techniques that make it easier for both subconscious processes and conscious interpretation.

Never word your question from the negative perspective. Let us imagine a situation in which a man is running for office in one of his clubs and wants to know the outcome. If he frames his question, "Will my opponent win the election?" or "Will I lose the election?" the subconscious can become confused between positive and negative reactions. If the man is fated to lose the election, the subconscious must reveal this misfortune with a white symbol, a color that has an association with happy events such as weddings and bridal finery. And if the man is to win the election, the subconscious must surface this happy news by presenting a black symbol, a color that has been associated with loss, grief, and misfortune throughout the ages as can be attested by widow's veils and mourning bands.

The correct framing of this question would be: "Will I win the office for which I am now running at the Writer's Club?" If the answer is *yes*, the subconscious can signal this good fortune with white. If the answer is *no*, the subconscious can signal this disappointment with black.

Note that the name of the club has been stated in the correctly worded dream programming. A man who belongs to several clubs is likely, as time goes by, to be involved in several elections. In fact, an emergency election might be held in another club before the election at the Writer's Club takes place. Also note how the word *now* pins down the time element. The questioner is interested in knowing the outcome of the present writer's club election, not one in which he may be running ten years from now.

If the proper wording of a question pertaining to the outcome of a forthcoming event seems perplexing, frame the question from the perspective of your own desire. Let us say that you have heard that your cousin Jane is coming to town and that you are wondering whether or not she will look you up. Do you want her to contact you? If so, word your question as: "Will cousin Jane come to see me on this trip as I am hoping?" But if you don't want to see your cousin, you could word your programming as follows: "Will I get out of having to entertain Jane when she comes to town next week?"

Guidance Questions

So far we have considered programming only questions of a prophetic nature, to learn how issues will be resolved in future time. Fortunately, we can also submit guidance questions such as, "Can I trust John as a business partner?" or "Shall I take the new job I have been offered in New York?"

We do not program these questions from the *wish* standpoint. We simply demand an answer as follows: "If I can trust John in business, give me a white symbol. If he is not to be trusted, give me a black symbol." And the new job offer would be programmed: "Should I take the new job I have been offered in New York? If so, give me a white symbol; if not, give me a black symbol."

The black and white dream symbol method can also give guidance when we must make a choice between two issues. Let us say that you have been offered a position that would locate you either in London or in Paris and that you wish to know which choice is the better. Decide which city appeals to you the most, say Paris, and program as follows: "Is the Paris job location the right choice? If so, give me a white symbol. If not, give me a black symbol."

Do not overwork the black and white symbol method. At the most, it should be used only once or twice a month.

Avoid These Mistakes

Many amateurs make the mistake of asking for a black or white symbol and then letting some aspect of this symbol other than its color influence their interpretation. A student had to decide whether or not to change from the morning shift on the switchboard of a certain police department to one that started at nine P.M. Although the evening shift carried a raise, the student felt she should be with her children during those hours. She asked to know whether, when all factors were considered, she should take the evening shift.

The next day she informed me that she had dreamed of white eggs turning on a spit. "But I am not going to take the evening shift," she protested, "because the eggs in the dream all had cracks in them." A short time later she wished she had taken the evening shift, for the person who took it was promoted to a day shift position superior to that of switchboard operator. The cracking of the eggs in this dream simply represented my student's fears for her children should she leave them in the care of another while she was on the night shift.

Another student asked if it was psychologically safe for her to program her dreams. She reported that she had dreamed of an old woman with white hair. But she interpreted the dream negatively because the old woman was unpleasant and menacing. This student was in the hospital with a lung infection at the time she made the experiment. It is little wonder that her dream content was unpleasant.

Before putting major decisions to the black and white dream programming method, test your accuracy. Select questions you know will be resolved within a short length of time and keep a record. In 1961 I wrote a monograph on the black and white dream method and advertised it in national magazines in order to test it among greater numbers of people. Over several years, hundreds of people sent letters of praise. I did not receive a single complaint. However, when I introduced the method in the Applied ESP Research Society that I have founded, one person out of a class of twenty found that the black and white dream signals do not predict correctly for her. I think this is due to a psychological block, for this student is one of the occasional individuals who can't read my card systems for herself, though she reads well for others.

Because ESP is a mental process, there is no such thing as a psychic or an ESP system that is 100 percent accurate. Even chess champions do not win every chess game, and great mathematicians do not work all problems correctly all the time. The human mind does not work in any area—objective or subjective—with an infallible continuity. This chapter has presented a paradox, for if the unconscious is all-knowing, it must know our intent even when we program a question vaguely such as "Will I win the election?" Why then is it wise to program more specifically, giving the name of the club and the present time element?

The answer lies in the fact that the reception or generation of ESP, whichever the case may be—and then the transmission to some form of conscious perception—is a highly complex operation in which aberrations can be caused, not only by psychological blocks, but also by a lack of coordination between levels of the ESP process—perhaps between preconscious and unconscious functions.

In my book, *The Cybernetic ESP Breakthrough*, I isolated divinatory aberrations such as emotional pull. I also listed *parallel presentations*. I must explain parallel presentations here, for they relate to improper programming in dreams as well as in card reading. Fortunately, I have a better understanding of this aberration today than when I wrote *The Cybernetic ESP Breakthrough*, and I am able to present an analysis of parallel presentations that can help my readers understand why we must program concisely.

Several years ago, the issue of abolishing capital punishment appeared on California ballots. I wanted to ascertain, via the cards, whether or not this measure would pass. Accordingly, I programmed a card with the words "chances capital punishment will be abolished." Then I slipped this specially programmed card into a deck programmed with my *associative card code*, shuffled the cards, and laid them out in the correct pattern to be studied. I saw clear indications that the measure would pass. In fact, I saw newspaper headlines and radios and televisions blaring forth this news.

I went to the telephone to record this prediction on a dated Western Union wire. But seconds before my hand touched the receiver, something deep and wise arose in my consciousness and flashed a warning—"No! Don't!"—and I obeyed. When the election was held in California the next day, the measure to abolish capital punishment was defeated. But a day or two later, newspapers, radios, and televisions were blaring forth the news that capital punishment had been abolished in New York!

This experience led me to theorize that ESP may operate on more than one mind level: (1) the all-knowing level, the level that prevented me from recording an erroneous prediction that California would abolish the death penalty; and (2) another level that had been blind to any intention of mine over and above the writing on the specially programmed card— "chances capital punishment will be abolished." Evidently this mind level had processed data until it had either found or figured out a future situation corresponding to the programmed message. Then it had mechanically arranged this data during the shuffle.

It is this mechanical blindness that may give us a clue to

parallel presentations. Perhaps the data processing department of the mind may occasionally jump ahead of another department that is capable of a total truth evaluation that is not limited to the written programming, but which knows the full intention of the person programming the question. In these instances, it may be that the power of suggestion is at fault. Popular dream books and coded card reading systems all carry a suggestion that the subconscious minds of most of us are capable of carrying out a presentation of paranormally gained information. A specific written programming may be a more powerful suggestion than a thought held in mind. And a suggestion implanted in the human mind will work blindly and mechanically to achieve its purpose with a high disregard for the intention of the individual involved. We see instances of this in the phenomenon of hypnosis when those under trance, or reacting to posthypnotic suggestion, mechanically and blindly carry out instructions that make them the laughing stock of others. Since it is evident that the process of programming the mind to present black and white dream signals is a feat of suggestion, we must make this suggestion exact when the circumstances around our question demand such precision.

Dream Book Training

When you purchase your coded dream books, place them on a table free of other objects. Seat yourself at this table and look at the books as you activate the levels of your inner mind with the suggestions listed below. Repeat each suggestion several times, two or three times a day, until you begin to receive dream symbols that predict the future or give guidance in accord with the interpretations given in the books. Reinforce the suggestions by pointing to your solar plexus area while speaking to your inner mind as though it were an entity separate from yourself.

1.   Attention, inner mind levels. During dreams you will

guide and protect me by using the symbols given in these books.

2.   Inner mind levels! You can and do present symbols from these dream books that will predict future events.

3.   Attention, inner mind. You can and do fade out nonessentials in my dreams while bringing meaningful dream symbols into strong focus.

4.   Attention, inner mind levels. You can and do inter-weave associative processes and dream book symbols into meaningful messages that I can interpret.

There are several methods other than pointing to the solar plexus area that are good reinforcement techniques: (1) repeat the suggestions aloud; (2) make a tape recording and listen to the suggestions as they are played back; (3) imagine that you hear a voice repeating the suggestions; (4) write out the suggestions; or (5) after you have written out the suggestions, retrace them by going over each word lightly with a pencil.

General Suggestions

The following list of suggestions has been designed to influence both conscious and subconscious mental levels toward the production and understanding of ESP dreams:

1.   I always remember my ESP dreams.

2.   My sleeping habits adjust to produce more ESP dreams.

3.   My conscious mind level and my inner mind levels work together to produce ESP dreams.

4.   I become more and more able to understand how my ESP dreams relate to my affairs.

5.   I always know when a dream answers a question I have in mind.

6.   My ESP dreams become outstanding and easy to remember.

7.   I receive ESP dreams that save me and my loved ones from mistakes and accidents.

8.   Whenever necessary I have ESP dreams that warn me away from mistakes and transgressions.

9.   During sleep I often achieve a state of consciousness that is conducive to ESP dreams.

10.   All my mind levels work in harmony to produce ESP dreams and hunches.

11.   My dreams and hunches alert me to opportunities and help me make right decisions.

12.   My ESP faculty grows strong and controls my other mental processes whenever this is necessary for my safety or edification.

Work with two or three of the above suggestions three times a day, if possible. When the list is exhausted, work on any of the suggestions that are the most needed.

The Master Suggestions

Before doing any type of programming, whether for a specific matter, dream book training, or working toward a general upgrading of ESP dreams, point to the solar plexus area and awaken the inner mind with the following master suggestions:

1.   My programming is effective. My programming works.

2.   When I implant a suggestion, it reaches the proper mind levels and produces results.

3.   Every facet of my mind that has been designed to carry out my suggestions is now alert and at attention, open and receptive to my commands.

4.   My inner mind always hears my commands, and it always obeys.

5.   I am making the following suggestions for only one reason. They are to be acted upon, and to my advantage.

Techniques of Indirect Suggestion

Up to this point, I have dealt with programming using

techniques of direct suggestion. However, there are methods that use the power of indirect suggestion to influence the mind toward true dreaming. In these techniques, we do not "talk" to the inner mind or program or issue suggestions. We allow the conscious, subconscious, and unconscious processes a chance to absorb possibilities and make their own synthesis. The subconscious and unconscious processes of the mind are capable of a surprising degree of logical initiative and originality. As a builder of card codes, I am often amazed that the hidden mind levels can achieve messages in ways that had not occurred to me consciously. Dream ingenuity is equally rewarding.

After you have given your inner mind levels suggestions for using books of coded dream symbols, place these books on a table or nightstand beside your bed. Why? So that your inner mind will associate them with sleep and dreams. This is the first example of indirect programming for ESP dream productions.

And this book you are now reading is, in itself, so powerful an agent for activating the dream faculty that many have only to read it in order to produce meaningful dreams. During the seven years that I worked intermittently on this book, I observed an acceleration of ESP dreams whenever the manuscript was reread and writing resumed. Typists and secretaries who worked on the manuscript began to experience ESP dreams even though they had not engaged in the psychic exercises presented in the previous chapter. The reason for this phenomenon is not hard to detect. The various mind levels are activated as their roles in ESP dreams are discussed, and the dreams that illustrate these functions are true case histories that are catalytic examples.

Read this book until you understand it thoroughly, and then keep it beside your bed with your coded dream books so that your mind levels will be given a strong, indirect suggestion to produce ESP dreams.

There is still another book that you should keep on your nightstand—the Bible, that great archetypal record, which is in itself an archetype, deeply etched in every mind. Even the agnostic and the atheist are subconsciously impressed. I have devoted the last chapter of this book to the true Biblical position on ESP for two reasons: (1) the texts to which I refer should help erase any trace of guilt that has been imposed by the erroneous concept that the Bible bans all divinatory procedures; and (2) many laws underlie the activation of the ESP faculty or faculties. One is the *law of psychic transference* or the *law of psychic contagion*. This law is one of the great Biblical themes. Saul became a prophet by fraternizing with other psychics (1 Samuel, chapter 10). And this law was in operation when Moses shared the blessings of prophecy with members of his congregation (Num. 11:24-28) and when Paul laid hands on the congregation at Ephesus (Acts 19:2-6).

Bible students often become highly intuitive through the *law of psychic contagion*, for the Bible is the only history that recognizes man's proclivity for ESP and gives it due credit as a natural mechanism that works in favor of survival and then progresses to creativity and the heights of spiritual awareness.

Creating a Psychic Environment

Many who read this book can take advantage of the law of psychic contagion by creating a group psychic environment. A family group project is a good start that can be extended to include relatives outside the immediate family circle as well as friends. Ask members of your family to confide their dreams so that you can interpret for them. In some instances, you will find that the dreamer has not dreamed exclusively for himself but has received a warning or found a problem solution for another family member or for the family as a total unit. Your own appearance in the dreams of other family members can give you many ESP messages. Teach family members the black and white dream symbol programming technique taught in this chapter, and work on family questions and problems as a group.

Ask your friends to tell you their dreams so that you can interpret for them. At birthdays and at Christmas, give this book as a gift so that relatives and friends can have the blessing of understanding their dreams. When they give you an account of their ESP dreams and the way they worked out, your own inner mind levels will be inspired toward ESP dreaming. There is also the advantage of your own position in the ESP dreams of your friends. Usually, when a friend relates a dream in which I am one of the figures, I can find an association with my own affairs that the friend knows nothing about, and I often receive valuable information.

Teach yourself and your family my card reading methods, and introduce them to your friends so that you can exchange readings. The cards act to accelerate the dream faculty, and the exchange of these readings aids the reception of helpful hunches and impressions. My method of reading the tarot is a catalyst for beneficial psychic development, especially dreams and the sighting of objectified dream symbols during waking hours, for I have coded in accord with the archetypal patterns that these cards activate in the human mind.

As your group grows, you may wish to hold meetings once a week or twice a month. The exercises in the previous chapter and the programming suggestions given in this chapter can become group projects that are followed by an exchange of dream interpretations and card readings, for these pursuits work together to create a psychic environment that can be interesting and beneficial to all concerned.

A Winning Regime

The person reading this book now has a dynamic battery of

ESP dream techniques at his command. Below is a summary:

1. The exercises taught in Chapter 12.
2. The dream book training, general programming, and master programming taught in Chapter 13.
3. The indirect programming methods taught in Chapter 13.
4. The recording of dreams in a dream diary.
5. The immediate attempt to decipher each dream through dream book codes and association.
6. The analysis of the dream to determine whether it relates to moral guidance, present situations, or to coming events.
7. A long-range observation of dreams recorded in the diary to ascertain whether or not they predicted future events.
8. The creation of a psychic environment.

After recognizable ESP dreams are produced, there may be fallow periods. If such a condition persists for several months, this book should be read again; if meaningful dreams do not result, the training regime outlined above should be resumed.

14

How to Make
Multiple Choice Selections

No one has less natural interest in the race tracks than I. Certainly I have not devoted my life to developing systems of applied parapsychology to encourage gambling. I believe that our ESP faculties should be devoted to life's highest purposes: the protection of our loved ones and ourselves; guidance to opportunities through which we can develop mentally and spiritually as we prosper; leadings to our rightful work and purpose in life through avenues of service to others. Believe me, this is the only way to win in the game of life.

However, the races were included in my research because they were the ideal target for multiple choice experiments. In the previous chapter, I gave you a simple method for determining the better choice between two situations, but making choices from three or more prospects is a much greater feat of ESP. The second reason I chose to research the races is that hits or misses can be tabulated right away without the waiting periods involved with personal or national and international predictions.

There was, however, a greater payoff from the races for me than the convenience of an immediate target appraisal. I learned much about ESP in general, and dreams in particular, that I shall now pass along to you. Also, this chapter allows me the economy of introducing important aspects of ESP as the racetrack research is presented. Here is a list of the fascinating topics to be revealed—valuable ESP knowledge that can be applied to many life situations:

1.   How to create daytime associations that can aid the dream to reveal the right selection in a multiple choice situation.

2.   The high ESP content of hypnagogic (the state just before sleep) and hypnopompic (the state just before waking) dreams.

3.   The ESP value of words spoken in a dream.

I first chose the races as a target while researching an adaptation of Rorschach-type blots to ESP purposes. I was very naive about the races, but I did know enough to purchase racing forms, and I studied them for a short time before beginning the project. I noticed that twelve races were always run at Tijuana, Mexico, and that only seven horses were entered in the fifth race, whereas as many as twelve horses were often scheduled for other races. I decided to make the fifth race the target because the fewer the horses the better the chances to make ESP hits. Then I formed a group of seven, including myself, all of whom were as ignorant as I about racing, and we turned our attention to the fifth race that was to be run in Tijuana the following Saturday.

I gave each person, including myself, a sheet of typing paper and assigned each of us the name of a horse, which we wrote at the top of our papers. Then we all folded the papers down the center and reopened them. Next, we dipped medicine droppers into bottles of various colored inks and let the ink fall to the papers as we kept turning them with our left hands. Finally, we refolded the papers and ran our fingers lightly over the upturned side to distribute the ink. But the most important part of the procedure was concentrating upon whether or not the horse we had been assigned would be the winner. Then the blots were opened so that we could all study them.

To our amazement, five of the blots, in their total concept, depicted horse faces! More than this, three of the specimens contained pictures of detached horse legs and hoofs, forms we had never before seen in blots though most of us had made hundreds of them. Another peculiarity was that two of the blots contained Chinese faces. Using the key of the *play upon words,* I decided that the Chinese faces predicted defeat and that the horses whose names were written at the top of these papers did not have a "Chinaman's chance" to win. I was right.

As it happened, we picked a winner. However, I am sure this was just a lucky fluke. It is fortunate that we wagered all our money "on paper," for we did not pick a winner during the next six times that the group got together. However, we were coming closer, for I was observing signs, such as the detached legs and hoofs that indicated losers. I am sure our subconscious minds were trying to set up a coded frame of reference with which we could detect winners or losers. But people with a genuine interest in researching ESP from the standpoint of parapsychology are seldom interested in gambling, and our group was typical. Three of the group had to leave the city, and those of us who remained were finding the blots so fascinating in areas of personal, national, and international predictions that we lost interest in the races. I closed the research project by encasing the blot specimens that had formed horses' faces and hoofs in cellophane and filing them away to be shown during lectures, for I considered them valuable evidence that the conscious mind can influence a subconscious production.

Eighteen months later, a man who had attended a lecture at which the collection of racing blots had been shown called me on the telephone. He reported that he had had some success in picking racehorse winners with his own ESP ability, and he wanted me to reopen my research with the blots. As I have stated before, I do not find the races intriguing. I declined. But that night I had a dream destined to rekindle my interest in researching the horses.

I was visiting the high school from which I had been graduated, talking with a teacher (long dead, but not in the dream) with whom I had been a favorite. "Do you remember little Margie?" she asked. "She is doing very well in life. She married well. Her husband just bought her a new fur coat." (At this point in the dream a strong visual impression of a coat of pony fur came into sharp focus and then faded out as the teacher resumed her conversation.) "And the child is becoming prominent in politics. She is running for the office of state controller."

I awakened and jotted down the dream, but it had no significance for me. I could find no association with the previous day, so I thought the dream was nothing more than a simple wish fulfillment to revisit my old school and learn about friends. Later in the day when I picked up my pad to review the dream, I began to wonder why the coat had been of *pony* fur. I decided to seek a clue in the spoken words of the dream and discovered *running*. Finally realizing that the dream was an association with the previous day, I called the man who had expressed a desire to research the races with me to find out whether or not a horse named "Margie" might soon be running. There was no horse named Margie on his racing form, but there was a horse in the fifth race named *"Political Plum"* that he thought would come in first when the fifth race was run on the following Saturday, and this proved to be the case.

If this dream was precognitive, and I am sure it wasn't

mere chance, my subconscious, which had been trained to present winners from the fifth race during the making of blots, had been triggered by the phone call to revert to the habit of processing the fifth race to determine the winner, but this time through my dreams! To test this theory, I bought a racing form and instructed my subconscious to pick another winner, through the agency of a dream, for the fifth race that was to be run the following Saturday. I did this programming without referring to the racing sheet.

That night I dreamed I was again a young woman of twenty and still working in a furniture store in which I had a financial interest. I was in the midst of making a sale when my pencil broke, and I had to go to the office for another. On the bookkeeper's desk, I found a crumpled old paper bag that contained three white pencils. As I selected one, the dream faded.

As I have stated in a previous chapter, sex symbols can be very meaningful in ESP content. Here we have two of these symbols, the paper bag (a female sex symbol) and the pencils (phallic sex symbols), which combined to indicate a winner. I studied the racing sheet and picked *Manchero*, who was to oblige me by coming in first. I made this choice through two associative clues. The crumpled paper sack was a replica of a bag I had once seen filled with money; the symbol *man* was associated with the phallic symbolism and reinforced by the symbol of the womb (the sack) from which *man* comes forth.

At this point in my research, I decided to vary the experiment by looking at the racing forms before commanding myself to dream. When I did this, I discovered that some of the names of the horses were so long or so odd that it would be difficult to make an association even if I did dream a winner. I decided to solve this problem by breaking the long and odd names down to more simple terms. For example, one horse was named *Ladrillo*. I broke the name down to three key words with which my dream faculty might work—*lad, drill* and *ill*. At half-hour intervals during the day, I reviewed the names of the horses and their key words. At the conclusion of these exercises, I commanded my subconscious to present a dream that would reveal the winner.

That night I had two dreams that associated with the word *ill*, and one of these dreams was about a *lad*. The first dream featured a coat and a pair of gloves I had once owned. Both the coat and the gloves had been worn during a period of my life when I was very *ill*. The second dream was about a little *lad* who had played with my son when he was three years old and undergoing a period of *ill* health. In the dream, I was fitting a space helmet on the head of my son's old playmate, but the helmet turned into a *medicine cabinet*. Both the dreams associated with the word *ill* in *Ladrillo*. Yes, Ladrillo was the winner!

A study of the four dreams I have just recounted revealed that my subconscious was reverting to associations of past years in order to obey my commands. What would happen, I wondered, if I reinforced the names of the horses, or their key words, with associations provided the day before I intended to dream? This procedure would cater to the natural inclination of dreams to utilize associative material from the past forty-eight hours. Would it enable my dream faculty to present the winners more clearly? I decided to find out. As you study my record, remember that this system can be applied to situations other than the races.

I deliberately associated the names of the horses that were to run in the fifth race the next Saturday with familiar objects that were in the house. For instance, one horse had a peculiar name that I can't recall—something like Pyenellius—anyway, it began with the syllable *pye* that can be associated with *pie*. During the day I concentrated on a custard pie I had in the refrigerator, and I paid special attention to it whenever I had to open the refrigerator door.

In this same race was a horse named *Viceregent*. I found a

pair of *dice* in the house with which I set up the association of *vice*. As I did this, I recalled that the word *vice* or *vise* designated a tool, and the expression "caught in a vise" ran through my mind. However, I did not have a vise with which to make a deliberate association. The names of the other horses running in the race I wished to predict were easy to associate with household objects.

At intervals during the day, I looked at and touched all the reinforcement objects while issuing the command that my subconscious pick a winner by associating with the right object and presenting it in a dream.

That night I had two dreams. In the first, I tried to enter an elevator but got caught between the doors—an association with the words *caught in a vice*—a very Freudian manipulation of being "caught in a vise." And as the second dream incriminates me still further, I will only state that I woke myself up shouting: *"Custard pie! Pie! Pie!"*

Pyenellius—or whatever that odd name is—won the race.

The fact that I had dreamed two possible winners was disconcerting. Today I know more about the way I dream and about dreams in general. The custard pie dream had two indications in its favor: (1) it was hypnopompic; and (2) it featured the spoken word.

Accredited laboratory parapsychologists who specialize in dream research have learned that dreams occurring as one first drifts from the waking to the sleeping state (hypnagogic dreams) and dreams occurring between sleeping and waking (hypnopompic dreams) are often more rich in ESP content than ordinary dreams. My own research corroborates these findings. The custard pie dream was definitely hypnopompic, occurring just before my usual waking time, and very dimensional, as most of my hypnagogic/hypnopompic dreams are.

I have learned to listen to dream words spoken by myself or others. We have an example of the value of the spoken word in the first dream recorded in this chapter in which the words of my old school teacher contained a veiled lead to "Political Plum." I am happy that I have developed methods that make the spoken word much more forthright, as in the custard pie dream, so that interpretation does not have to be used.

In my case, and I think it will be found to be generally true, my dreams soon refused to handle the races. Here we find an analogy in psychoanalytic dreaming. After the subconscious presents a few significant dreams for the analyst, it usually loses interest and reverts to ordinary dreams. *We must never overload the dream faculty with dream commands or deliberate programming.* I am sure that had I waited two or three months and then resumed my program of instructing my subconscious to pick winners at the races it would have done so, for some of my students report success in rekindling the interest of the subconscious in overworked questions after a period of time has elapsed.

15

The Paranormal
Wish Fulfillment

I shall begin this chapter by coining a term for a dream component with which our psychologists and dream experts will someday become familiar—the *paranormal wish fulfillment*. The term refers to the gratification of one of man's greatest desires, the wish to see his own affairs and also the universal scheme in a greater perspective than that afforded by the known senses. Throughout this chapter I shall refer to this desire as "the wish to perceive paranormally."

It is little wonder that wish fulfillment is the basic objective of our dreams, for this principle is the dominating factor in creating the reality in which we live and move while awake. When hunger assails us, we wish to alleviate its pangs with food, and thus nature assures the survival of the individual. When the tensions of sex build up, sometimes to the point of pain, this biological process compels the wish for relief, and thus the preservation of the race is assured. Fortunately, nature has goals in mind for man other than his mere existence and propagation. The basic wishes to relieve pain and obtain pleasure lead to the development of the soul. Every poem, every piece of sculpture, every musical score, and every cathedral are materialized wishes.

Man's first artistic production was the dream. Freud's observation that the dream is usually instigated by a latent or overt sexual desire has been borne out in recent years by an interesting series of experiments conducted by psychiatrists. A few seconds before rapid eye movements (REM) signal that a dream has started, male subjects experience a penile erection that generally continues throughout the REM period, diminishing gradually as the subject moves out of the dream state.

Long before the sexual origin of the dream was discovered, the analytical, almost intuitive genius of Freud linked sex libido to all forms of creativity. He called this principle *sublimation*. What a beautiful attribute of man. He cannot live by sex alone but must sacrifice a great portion of the sex drive in the interests of the arts and sciences that benefit and exalt the race. It is true that some of this libido must be expended for necessary food and shelter, but history tells us that the arts and sciences were born in climatically mild and fertile places such as the Nile Valley and Greece where man could have spent much of his time in revelry instead of the creative and idealistic pursuits to which he so often turned.

Jung had to forego the principle of sublimation in his objection to some of Freud's facts of life concerning the sexual aspects of psychology. But the sublimation theory is partially present in Jung's psychological philosophy that the prime goal of man is "wholeness," which can only come about through the principle of *individuation*. And, characteristic of Jung, individuation is an introverted process, a striving to find and perfect the self through a study of one's dreams. This task requires psychiatric help since the average man, according to Jung, does not have the in-depth knowledge required for his own dream analysis. It goes without saying that Jung's "wholeness" is a desirable condition, not only for the individual, but also for the race, for such a balance would prevent the misdirection of energy and turn it into constructive channels. But even without achieving this "wholeness," man is set upon accomplishment. Jung's life is a case in point.

Before his death he admitted that he was still a sadly confused man, even more unsure of himself or of the pinpointing of any universal truth than before his extensive study of the sciences and philosophies. He never did reach his desired "wholeness," but his striving toward this state required a *sublimation* of libido energy that enabled him to make a contribution to the world.

It is little wonder that Jung considered dream analysis beyond the scope of the average education. When his inability to face his own dream psychology caused him to repudiate Freud's theory of latent wish fulfillment, Jung had to postulate a substitute to explain away and replace this phenomenon. He attempted to structure a dream process that he referred to as the *principle of compensation*—a theory as nebulous as the fabled emperor's nonexistent clothes. As an analytic technique it can only be used, said Jung, by the psychologist whose education has been augmented by an extensive knowledge of mythology, folklore, the psychology of primitives, and comparative religion. Furthermore, said Jung, there are no set rules by which we may pinpoint the operation of compensation. While the theory is so universal that we are now beholding it in the subjective art forms and literature that are a protest against the objective reality of our materialistic age, it differs so widely in individuals that it can seldom be recognized!

It is fortunate, indeed, that neither analytical psychology nor the new science of parapsychology needs the principle of compensation in order to decipher messages of the dream. Freud's theory of wish fulfillment is the correct tool in both instances. The wish fulfillment purpose of dreams is so valid that, in accord with dream condensation, it can sometimes operate on three levels of a single dream—supplying a latent wish fulfillment, a simple wish fulfillment, and a paranormal wish fulfillment. The *Wedding Preparation Dream* in Chapter 7 is a good example of a threefold wish fulfillment achievement.

Dreams that occur on the same night are usually quite different in manifest content. However, our psychologists know that they are often instigated by the same wish. A paranormal wish fulfillment can also influence dreams occurring on the same night, as the next two dreams to be presented will indicate. At the time of these dreams, tickets to Disneyland had been purchased for a family group consisting of my daughter, her husband, their four children, and my husband and myself. I was looking forward to the adventure, for I had long wanted to observe my grandchildren's first enjoyment of this fantastic amusement park. But I was also a bit apprehensive for, though I said nothing to my family, I was not feeling well. I have never been robust since a severe case of scarlet fever, and I feared that walking about the huge park would overtax my strength even though I might be feeling better. Two days before the trip, I went to bed feeling very disappointed because I had concluded that it would be best for me to stay at home. Then I experienced two dreams that were to change my mind.

Dream I—The Converted Hearse Dream. I was looking at a very odd car—a large, beat-up old hearse that had been converted into a station wagon. It had been painted a gay, bright blue with a band of dark blue around the lower portion of the chassis.

Dream II—The Japanese Children Dream. I was in Japan admiring the kimonos of a mother and two children—a boy of eight and a girl of six. The mother handed the boy two tickets. He studied them for a moment, then threw them down on the ground, and stomped on them before he marched off.

When I attempted to analyze the *Converted Hearse Dream*, I recalled that psychologists often relate the condition of a dream car to the dreamer's own body. This comparison made sense, for I am sixty-two years old and functioning in a damaged body that has narrowly escaped death on several occasions. The fact that the death car had been converted into a passenger vehicle was a fortunate omen. Also, the car had been painted blue, a color that denotes healing in my code.

The *Japanese Children Dream* shed more light on the *Converted Hearse Dream*. According to the dream book I was consulting, Japanese people denote a pleasurable diversion from life's usual routine. This clue told me that the children and the tickets in the dream must relate to Disneyland. I knew I was being urged to go, and I knew that the blue paint on the converted hearse of the first dream meant that I would suffer no ill effects.

The prediction was true. I was feeling much better on the day slated for Disneyland. And when we arrived, I learned that my family had no intention of allowing me to walk all day. They rented a wheelchair and ordered me into it, allowing me out only for rides and meals. And so I enjoyed the long, exciting day at Disneyland with no ill effects.

The paranormal feature of the two Disneyland dreams extended beyond the wish fulfillment that I had been able to recognize in them. When my husband and I arrived at the Disneyland parking lot, we pulled up beside a very odd vehicle. A group of hippies were tumbling out of the same dilapidated converted hearse I had seen in my dream. It was painted a vivid, bright blue with the exception of a dark blue band around the lower fourth of the chassis!

There were also prophetic elements in the second dream. The Disneyland attraction that my six-year-old grand-daughter liked best was "It's a Small World," which is a gliding boat ride through a maze of animated dolls representing children of all countries. She was particularly thrilled by the Japanese dolls, and when she pointed them out to me, I was reminded of my dream of two nights before. Late in the day we had exhausted our supply of tickets except for the merry-go-round and the "Dumbo" ferris wheel. My eight-year-old grandson is usually a well-mannered boy, but when my daughter handed him his two remaining tickets, he was so disappointed in the "baby" rides they offered that he threw them down on the ground and then strode off to a bench in a huff.

Can a dream foreshadow a wish that is not yet entertained in the conscious state? One September day in 1970, my daughter told me a dream she had experienced the previous night—a nocturnal production that was to have strange psychic ramifications.

The Green Robe Dream. My daughter lifted a beautiful robe of shimmering green from a gift box and tried it on. As she admired the lovely garment, one of our deceased relatives —an aged woman who had objected to the adoption of my daughter and who had never liked her—came into the room, demanding the robe. When my daughter refused, the aged woman tried to take the robe off her, and they tussled for it. I came into the room and advised my daughter to humor the old lady and let her have the robe. My daughter did so reluctantly.

After three months had passed, the dream was forgotten. The bright cheer of the Christmas season was dimmed for our family because my daughter was having symptoms of a mastoid condition for which she had had two operations previously. Her specialist was treating her in the hope of avoiding a third operation but did not know which way the matter would be decided. However, I decided to buy my daughter a new robe for Christmas to cheer her during her convalescence in case she did have to have the operation. My husband and I went to a fashionable department store where a clerk seated us and brought robes for our inspection. We liked a beautiful rose-colored robe, but the clerk discovered that it was not my daughter's size. She went back to the rack where she discovered a green robe in the same style and shimmering material. After a consideration of just a few seconds, my husband and I decided to buy this robe.

I watched as the deft girl at the wrapping station shook the garment expertly. Air was retained in the robe, filling it out like a body, and as it lay upon the table with the wrapping clerk working over it, it seemed to foreshadow my daughter, helpless and limp on the operating table. There was no longer any doubt in my mind that the third operation would have to be performed.

When Christmas came, my daughter was pleased with the robe. She confided that she had been wishing for a long robe, for hers were all too short for hospital corridors. Two weeks later, my daughter had her third mastoidectomy, which resulted in a considerable loss of hearing in the afflicted ear. Her specialist wanted to perform a fourth operation—an experiment that might or might not restore lost hearing. However, I advised my daughter not to have surgery again. She was able to live normally with the hearing she had left, and I felt she had gone through too much suffering as it was.

During all this time, we forgot about my daughter's dream of the green robe. Then one day I ran across the dream in my files and realized how predictive it had been.

The green robe represented my daughter's hearing. The aged woman who had always caused trouble for my daughter during her lifetime also represented the hearing loss, for she, too, had lost the hearing in one ear from a mastoid condition. My advice to let the aged woman have the robe represented the advice I was to give later about foregoing the operation that might have resulted in a build-up of auditory perception. The green robe was also a realistically true dream fragment.

My daughter's recitation of the dream had nothing to do with the selection of a *green* robe through suggestion, for I had preferred a rose robe that was not the right size. However, my intuition that my daughter would have to have the operation, when I saw the air-inflated green robe on the wrapping table, was very likely triggered by a subconscious memory of my daughter's dream, which I had forgotten consciously and which I failed to remember until reminded of it months later.

Interesting though all the above speculation about the *Green Robe Dream* is, here we are mainly concerned with the theory that the ESP dream determinant may sometimes perform its predictive work by diverting the wish fulfillment element to a wish that is not to be entertained in consciousness until a later date. Such a situation would be a full-fledged paranormal wish fulfillment.

I realize, of course, that psychologically the *Green Robe Dream* must be classified as an ego dream in which the simple wish fulfillment is a general wish for pretty clothes. But as I have shown, the dream was prophetically associated with my daughter's ear condition in all its aspects, and for this reason I believe that the paranormal wish made the general wish specify a green robe. Unfortunately, one dream example does not establish a scientific fact. In the interest of a statistical record, I hope that any reader who dreams of a wish that was not entertained in consciousness until a later date—after which the dream did or did not come to pass (whichever was predicted by the dream material)—will get in touch with me.

The wish to perceive paranormally is so inherent in man that he is himself a divining instrument, as can be proved by a study of his dreams. More than this, the principle of divination within man can operate through artifacts that, like the dream, can produce meaningful subconscious productions. In previous chapters of this book, I have pointed out analogies between the dream and my divinatory methods of reading coded cards and Rorschach-type blots in the way that all three systems utilize the principles of arbitrary coding and associative processes. Here, I shall call attention to the way the paranormal wish fulfillment principle operates in all three systems.

As I have already taught, the wish to know paranormally has the ability to influence the dream in two ways: (1) a question held in mind will be answered; and (2) future events about which we have no present inkling will be shown. This is exactly the situation in coded card reading and Rorschach-type blots converted to ESP purposes. However, the dream, despite its proclivity for *condensation* most often represents only one purpose, either answering a question or presenting a future event, whereas the divinatory artifacts of cards or blots can perform both feats through either one shuffling of the cards or one dropping of ink, as the case may be. In fact, sometimes several of life's questions are answered and several future events are presented simultaneously in one card layout or in one blot. Perhaps this is because the dream is more psychologically impacted than the other two methods.

The card and blot methods also have the advantage of a wish that is held in mind at the time of operation. The will of the operator is in direct attendance, not acting upon a previous suggestion as is the case with the dream. And in card reading the wish to perceive paranormally can operate through a wish card, placing it with favorable cards if the wish is to be granted, or unfavorable cards if it is not. This device works with a remarkable ratio of accuracy because of the principle of the paranormal wish fulfillment.

Not just this last chapter but this entire book has been devoted to a study of the paranormal wish fulfillment of the dream and those factors and conditions that either further the ESP content or hinder or abort its achievements. In trying to track down the department of the mind most heavily relied upon by the ESP determinant, I have found, as this book plainly illustrates, that the preconscious does much of the paranormal work. This does not mean that I believe the preconscious to be the sole ESP determinant. The Italian psychoanalyst Emilo Servadio and his colleague Eugenio Gaddini have taken a stand that psi (ESP) dreams are not subjected to the elaborations of the unconscious but are transmitted intact. They rest their case on the fact that the preconscious, with its memory file, has the advantage of a certain organization, whereas Freudian psychology reveals the unconscious to be in a state of chaos.

Such a conclusion bypasses the fact that ESP is often dependent upon symbols from the unconscious, both in the case of the dream and in waking clairvoyance. It also bypasses Jungian psychology, which reveals the archetypes. Despite the fact that the archetypes often contaminate each other—as when an animus or anima is shadow-tinged—and despite the fact that the archetypes sometimes have complexes grouped around them, they contribute a structure of organization to the unconscious.

When we consider that a trained mind will use an arbitrary code to produce paranormal dreams, we are led to the conclusion that the preconscious is not the sole ESP determinant. These codes are not stored in the preconscious—at least not through any process of learning we now know. It is not necessary to memorize or even to scan a popular dream book before using it.

These facts strengthen the hypothesis that man may possess a superconscious mind, which as yet has not been incorporated into models of the human psyche by our psychologists. Such an ESP determinant would be able to sort out and choose material from even the chaotic aspects of the unconscious in the manner that case histories in this book demonstrate! Yet, in the final analysis, an ESP dream is always a partially conscious product—close enough to consciousness to be remembered—and, more often than not, there is an ego awareness almost as strong as in the waking state.

This ego identification in dreams is, however, more than consciousness carried over from the waking state. We must remember that, contrary to popular supposition, the ego is not just an objective awareness of the self. On the contrary, the structure of the ego begins in the unconscious and progresses through the preconscious before culminating in conscious awareness.

Here we have a clue that may answer an important question. In postulating a superconscious mind, where would we place it in the new model of the human psyche? I think it is a structure running through the total ego, capable of an operation that Jung ascribed to the human mind—not just a conscious ingestion sinking down into subconscious and unconscious levels, but a rising of original material made possible by the interaction of archetypes in both the personal unconscious and the collective unconscious. Such a path between conscious, preconscious, and unconscious associative processes would also account for the twin sister of ESP—creativity.

And, in the final analysis, what are the archetypes? Their existence is, to my mind, a *wish fulfillment*. Even the most hateful of the archetypes, the *shadow*, which we have projected upon the world as the devil who is responsible for all our woes, is high on the list of our desires, as our literature and drama show plainly. We are not interested in the story, novel, or drama that has no conflict. Our protagonist must face problems that can be resolved by winning, compromising, or losing—it does not matter which, for we lose interest and boredom sets in when there is no longer a form of conflict. We have the unconscious wish for problems because, at this point in our evolution, they are developing our abilities so that we may someday have greater desires and cope with greater issues.

The archetype of the *great mother* is both kind and cruel, having her origin in the example of "Mother Earth" who, as

Jung has pointed out, sustains us in life but claims us in death. The human mother must chastise as well as cherish. If she is too soft, she falls short of the wish fulfillment of nature for the production of a strong and enlightened generation.

Because I am a person with a trained capability to receive more paranormal dreams in a quarter of a year than most people do in a lifetime, I feel qualified to state that the full functioning of ESP that can be obtained through my dream methodologies is as natural an experience as the ordinary dream. The experience of an entirely natural occurrence is also the case when I shuffle and then lay out cards that have been coded to form messages.

Even when I am making my amazing national and international predictions, the process is as commonplace as shuffling for a bridge game and appraising the cards that fall into my hand. The only difference between shuffling cards for ESP messages and shuffling them for a game is my mode of concentration. When I shuffle for a game, I wish, of course, for a good hand for myself. When I shuffle cards for a reading, I exercise the wish to perceive paranormally toward a specific question, and, of course, I am also hoping (wishing) to obtain the spontaneous messages that usually occur along with details concerning the wish.

Unfortunately, there are instances when an emotional block interferes with the wish to perceive paranormally. In these cases, there is often a displacement of people, an aberration that makes a fully correct ESP message impossible. Whenever I dream that I am undergoing surgery, the event in real life is never for me but for my daughter or one of her children. In this case, perhaps a mother's wish to suffer in the stead of her children is gratified. I am always right about the type of surgery that will have to be performed, but I am emotionally prevented from seeing which loved one will have to experience this crisis.

In my files I have a most interesting case of a natural

psychic whose waking hunches are distorted by the displacement of persons. This psychic often blurts out a dire prediction to a friend or an acquaintance only to learn later that the warning was intended for a member of her own family. At one time during a telephone conversation with a neighbor, Ms. Brown said compulsively: "Don't take little Jimmy to the neighborhood supermarket in your car during the next two weeks. There is sure to be an accident in which the child will be hurt." The neighbor did not believe in ESP. She took her child to the store with her daily and without mishap. But eight days after the prediction, Ms. Brown's daughter and small grandson came for a visit. Late in the afternoon, the three got into the daughter's car and headed for the supermarket. There was an accident in which the grandchild was the only person injured.

On another occasion Ms. Brown was seated beside a strange man as she rode home on a bus after a day's shopping. She grew uneasy about the man's safety and felt compelled to tell him not to do any carpentry work during the next week for he would injure his left hand badly if he did. The stranger replied that he had to engage in carpentry the next week for he was a carpenter by trade, but he took Ms. Brown's telephone number and promised to report. The stranger worked through the next week without mishap. The accident was shaping up for Ms. Brown's son who smashed his left hand badly while adding a patio to his home.

Had Ms. Brown's premonitions been fully correct, in the above instances, she could have prevented two accidents.

Some who are gifted psychically consciously resent their ability because it so often depicts mishaps or tragedies. But if these people would develop their intuitions to their full capacity, many untoward events could be avoided or righted. Those of us who must augment our native hunch power through divinatory systems must also learn to be brave. As I have pointed out in *The Cybernetic ESP Breakthrough*, the blessed all-knowing functioning that can predict the trend of an unfortunate future event can often show us a solution. At one time both my cards and my dreams were filled with death predictions for my son. During the course of these dire warnings, my son became mysteriously ill, developing a staph condition that was not correctly diagnosed for three years because the symptom of fever was lacking. Finally the staph caused growths around the bladder, and they had to be removed surgically. This operation made the staph count still worse. Then one awful day my son's physician told me all that could be done for my boy was to make him comfortable and watch carefully for the symptoms of peritonitis that were sure to set in. Thoroughly alarmed, I questioned a friend who had a college degree in nursing and was studying to become an M.D. She told me that people in my son's condition are considered terminal. This opinion was confirmed when an acquaintance who had the same malady as my son passed away.

My days became a prayer without ceasing, and I would wake up at night with a plea for my son's life on my lips. One day a friend told me about an American physician who had gone to Mexico in order to use European therapies not yet approved in this country. I considered this man a quack, so I did not bother to program him into my cards or into my dreams. But a few mornings later, just as I was waking up, I had a vivid impression that my son was standing by my bed. "Mother," he said, "if you will take me to the American doctor across the border I can live."

I took my son to the American doctor in Mexico for treatment, and two months later, my son reported an upsurge of vitality and a feeling of comfortable well-being that he had not known for a long time. I then took him back to his original physician for a staph count. He was amazed by the radical change for the better that had taken place. Today my son is in good health, and his American physician reports that organs that were badly affected have rebuilt and are functioning normally.

The wish to perceive paranormally is directly related to a still higher type of wish for which man has a proclivity—the great archetypal ideals, which will be discussed in the next chapter.

16

The Archetypal
Wish Fulfillment

The dichotomy between Freudian and Jungian psychology became clearly defined when Jung introduced his concept of the archetypes. Jung asserted that dreams reveal the divine in man as well as the animal, and he proved this point by unveiling the archetype of the *hero*, a recurring theme in art and literature that led Jung to believe that man will evolve into a "semi-divine" being.

Both science and religious philosophy have a common goal: perfected man in a perfected environment. I believe that if such a stage is ever reached, it will be because man has a psychic potential that has been exemplified in the Bible. Whether or not we view Moses and Christ as actual historical figures or merely as idealized prototypes, they represent an aspect of the *hero* that is an archetype in its own right, the *magician*.

In fact, the Bible, itself, is a psychic literature from cover to cover. For example, Jesus was not entrusted to a nonpsychic.

In the New Testament we read that Joseph took Mary as his wife on the advice of a dream (Matt. 1:20). Later he saved Jesus from the wrath of Herod through a dream (Matt. 2:12).

Parapsychology, like all other sciences, must stand on its own merits without a doctrinal religious bias. However, religion is now within the province of parapsychology as an impersonal analytical project. From the scientific standpoint, parapsychologists cannot uphold the historical accuracy of the Judeo-Christian Scriptures. However, the psychic content of the Bible is consistent, revealing a well-ordered classification of phenomena that is not in conflict with modern findings. The Biblical laws of psychic prohibition and psychic permission are especially interesting. I shall first list and deal with the prohibitions:

1. Necromancy—the mediumistic attempt to conjure up the spirit of a dead person against his will in order to question him.

2. Endangering the body by attempting to walk through fire.

3. Black witchcraft or black magic with the intent of harming another.

4. The use of herbs or drugs in an attempt to achieve ESP.

5. The worship of a divinatory artifact.

6. The attempt to conjure up a heathen god, or a demon, or an evil spirit or force for purposes of ESP.

7. The use of dreams, astrology, or any form of ESP to further an evil cause.

8. Surrendering consciousness and body functions to an "unclean spirit."

After Moses and Paul put down evils such as those listed above, they considered it their mission to reeducate their congregations into rightful practices. We know that prophecy was not limited to the priesthood, for psychically gifted women were allowed to advise the people. In the Old Testament, Miriam and the great Deborah were sought out. And in the New Testament the prophetess Anna gave counsel at the temple. Furthermore, ESP was not limited to religious prophecy as many of us have been taught, but was also allowed for practical purposes. For instance, when a man named Kish could not find his beasts of burden, his son Saul went to consult Samuel and brought him a present, as was the custom (1 Sam. 9:3-20). The early Christians used ESP for practical purposes for centuries before the Western branch, which was under the jurisdiction of the Popes, prohibited this practice under pain of death.

Although this prohibition went to ridiculous lengths, even banning the study of mathematics to the clergy, it was no doubt imposed because evil and dangerous ESP practices had again become rampant.

Unfortunately, there are ESP methods that can endanger the mind. Both Ouija boards and automatic writing are unnatural physiological and mental processes during which the volition of the hands is surrendered to exteriorized energy while the subconscious spells or writes out messages. Only the psychically gifted can obtain a reasonable degree of accuracy. For the majority of people there is usually only a great deal of nonsensical advice, lies in answer to questions, and sometimes a lowered moral tone. Worse yet, these practices can sometimes result in the terrible symptoms that Fundamentalists attribute to "Demon possession" and that the Spiritualists refer to as "possession by an earth-bound spirit."

The psychiatrist, however, considers these symptoms to be the result of mental dissociation, and he treats these symptoms very effectively. First he relaxes the patient and induces feelings of well-being with tranquilizers. Next, he prescribes an objective physical program during which the patient engages in social activities such as badminton or folk dancing. Meanwhile he counsels the patient, bringing him to realize that he is not the victim of an evil spirit who took over his hand to spell out messages and then became abusive, but only the victim of his own repressions and his own exteriorized energy. When the patient becomes convinced of these facts, he is healed.

This realization is sometimes hard to bring about, for exteriorized energy, or motoricity, is not limited to pushing a Ouija panchette or a pencil. It can progress to administering pinches, blows, sexual orgasm, and even disturbances in the environment. But the records of psychic researchers afford psychiatrists treating "possession" some clinching arguments. Mediums in whose presence heavy objects move about were tested. In every case there was a weight loss when the mediums were weighed after séances. A medium who could produce raps was painted vermillion and tied to her chair. When raps were heard on the opposite wall the area was examined and tiny splotches of vermillion were discovered. Later, it was discovered at Duke University that some people have the power of telekinesis, the ability to influence the movement of objects.

I am not saying there is no such thing as possession by an uncarnate or discarnate entity. I am saying that, during twenty years of research, the twenty-two cases of possession that came to my attention were no more than repressions—sex repressions that had the earmarks of a certain type of dream—the sex nightmare that is tortuously punitive in exchange for the small degree of physical or psychological release that is allowed.

Not all cases of possession result from motoricity methods or any form of psychic endeavor. Four of the cases I studied resulted from the excitement of revival meetings! Here we are reminded of the waves of "demonism" that have swept through celibate nunneries. Like motoricity methods, some highly charged emotional religious experiences suggest the presence of discarnate and uncarnate entities, and some who are in a state of psychological or physical sex repression are not able to achieve a full sublimation. But most of the cases I studied resulted from the unnatural mental and physical processes involved in motoricity methods of ESP.

Fortunately, the Bible teaches the principles that allow us to achieve ESP without disturbing the mind. The dream, divined for worthy purposes, is the first Biblical example. It is a subconscious production achieved through a natural mental and physiological process, sleep. Later, it is studied in the conscious state through the principles of association and arbitrary coding. And when Joseph stirred the dregs of his divining cup (Gen. 44:1-15), he performed a natural physiological act that formed a subconscious production of symbols that could be deciphered through the principles of association and code. Moses claimed that divining instruments called Urim and Thummim were commanded by the Lord (Exod. 28:30; Lev. 8:5-8). These coded artifacts were operated by the natural physiological process of throwing them upon the ground where they were deciphered through ordinary objective thinking (Num. 27:21; 1 Sam. 14:40-43).

My card codes are based on the same natural principles as the biblically sanctioned methodologies. A subconscious production is achieved through the natural physiological act of shuffling. And as readers of this book now know, when the cards are laid out, they are deciphered through association and arbitrary coding, natural mental processes that do not disturb any department of the mind.

Some well-intentioned evangelists, who have never made a depth study of parapsychology, have spread the misconception that all forms of ESP, including the divination of dreams, card reading, and the tarot, can induce the terrible symptoms of mental dissociation they attribute to "demons." This is not true. I have taught these methodologies to thousands without receiving a single complaint. On the contrary, many have testified that their mental processes have been strengthened. The principles upon which our Biblical forefathers relied for a safe, high-accuracy ESP are eternal. And, aided by our present scientific knowledge, they may work even better today than they did centuries ago.

Today, with only a few exceptions, our Western branch of Christianity is upholding the new science of parapsychology. Clergymen are beginning to take the view that the Eastern branch of Christianity has always maintained—that ESP, like electricity, is a natural phenomenon that can be used for either good or evil purposes. Catholic priests are now evangelizing in favor of ESP, traveling about the country with the message that parapsychology and demonism are separate fields. For centuries, biblical texts in favor of ESP went unmentioned from the pulpits, and only texts condemning ungodly and unwise ESP practices were cited. Now the tide has changed. I have been joined in my research by Catholic priests and leaders of the Baptist and Methodist faiths and other conventional denominations who realize that there is a scientific aspect to ESP that can be attributed to the way the Creator designed the human mind.

And the Creator, through nature, designed the human mind so that it is able to attain a natural state of altered consciousness called the dream. After studying the ESP content of many dreams, and making successful telepathic experiments, some of our parapsychologists reasoned, quite logically though to a great extent erroneously, that an induced altered state of consciousness during the waking state might be the answer to ESP for everyone. In an effort to achieve this altered mental state, some parapsychologists experimented with drugs—fortunately, under expert supervision and for only a short time.

Although I am avid for parapsychological research, I had an instinct against drugs, for every moment of conscious thinking is precious to me. Also, I knew that drug experiments would be fruitless, for ESP is a natural process. I had observed that gifted psychics, with the exception of a few trance mediums, were not dependent upon a state of consciousness that differed noticeably from the norm. I was deep enough into my research to know that nonpsychics can achieve ESP during the day through subconscious productions that do not alter consciousness, at least not at the objective level. And I had learned that a clear, logically functioning conscious mind is necessary for a sustained, high-accuracy ESP through the natural manipulation of coded artifacts and even through dreams. My research had included a scrutiny of the hippie drug subculture, which has had an interest in the occult, even to black magic and satanism—a far cry from the scientific endeavors of parapsychology or the wholesome lifestyle and idealistic philosophy of mainstream psychics such as Ms. Jeanne Dixon. In the hippie cases I observed, efforts to induce ESP through drugs were pitiful. Even the psychically gifted lost their subconscious abilities as their objective thinking deteriorated.

Long before parapsychologists had become interested in inducing altered states of consciousness through drugs, it had been learned at Duke University that trance mediums could demonstrate ESP equally well in the normal state. Nevertheless, the scientific regime demands that every avenue of a reasonable theory be explored. When brain waves were discovered and classified, it was learned that alpha waves indicate mental and physical relaxation that was thought to be conducive to ESP. But again, parapsychologists were disappointed. Although the attainment of alpha waves through disciplined meditation was found to be of some physiological and psychological value, this altered state of consciousness was not the mass gratification of one of man's greatest wishes—*the wish to perceive paranormally.*

At first consideration, this wish to perceive paranormally seems to clash with another great archetypal desire—man's wish for free agency. Philosophers have been apprehensive that precognition may mean that man's destiny is so fated as to preclude the choices necessary to moral responsibility. The science of psychology has revealed that man is far more conditioned into his moral state than had been supposed previously, and extensive social studies have revealed a sad fact: underprivileged ghettos are cultural traps that breed low moral and achievement standards.

Such a conditioning impact by environment runs counter to man's image of himself, for his desire for free agency is so great that in the doctrines of most religions we find him taking full responsibility for his state of morality. Our Western conventional religious faiths are firmly based on the principle that each individual determines his own salvation either through his choice of works or through his choice of Christ as his personal savior. Among the millions of re-incarnationists, all suffering is attributed to the sins of a past life or to the desire to experience sensation instead of unity with God. A wish so great as man's desire for a wide expanse of free agency is bound to be fulfilled. My new sciences of applied parapsychology are paradoxical, for while they reveal man's destiny to be far more fated than he likes to suppose, at the same time they place a staff in his hand by which he can reach a new pinnacle of choice from which he often can shape and guide his destiny.

In the previous chapter, I recounted a dream that enabled me to save my son's life. Who can deny that this dream gave me an exercise of free agency above the norm?

ESP can become man's greatest tool in his battle to escape a warping environment. On the personal level, he can be guided to a higher path of destiny, to opportunities he might bypass otherwise and, as I have pointed out previously, often he can avoid or mitigate evil. More than this, ESP can reinforce the individual's moral values. In dreams, the ESP determinant can often influence a normal superego, as is the case when the image of my stepfather scolds me for conduct or attitudes that I am tempted to rationalize. And, during twenty years of extensive ESP research, I have noted the same moral values operating through coded card reading and Rorschach-type blots, the only exceptions being cases of great emotional pull. Some sitters are so desirous of illicit love affairs that they disregard warnings and continue to have the cards run, or blots made, on this question until a favorable answer is obtained. Many moral warnings through the agency of applied ESP methods are entirely unsolicited, not in the mind of a sitter, until I point them out in cards, blots, or dreams. At one time I was giving a research reading for a stranger, a man whose cards revealed that it was wrong for him to engage in the cruel and most unusual sport of cock fighting! For a minute or two, the attitude of this man was a defiant denial, then he slumped into his seat and confessed. The cards and blots of young people often warn them away from pills and marijuana.

As individuals rise through wise and moral ESP practices, society as a whole will be uplifted through a higher level of perception. When sciences of applied parapsychology become more highly evolved, far-reaching environmental factors, such as government policy, economics, and science, will often be arrived at through ESP.

As for the value of ESP to scientific fields, I have demonstrated it. Although my systems of applied parapsychology are in their swaddling clothes, not yet grown to the stature to which great scientific minds contributing from specialized fields can bring them, they can perform feats such as detecting trouble spots in our space flights before these anomalies appear in actual experience, and they can predict earthquakes as to place, time, and intensity. With an uncontrovertibly documented record such as this behind me, a nonpsychic, I foresee the day when science will not have to rely solely on the tedious trial-and-error laboratory experiments by which we are attempting to know the causes and curative agencies for complicated diseases that now plague mankind. In that day, our scientists will receive leads by programming their dreams, as well as using other methodologies that I have innovated, and their experiments will be conducted from this vantage point. Man will no longer be buffeted about by inescapable storms and earthquakes nor will he suffer accidents.

I firmly believe that ESP is one of the keys to man's desire for a better world as it is archetypally portrayed in the Book of Revelations. Man does not wish to grapple with his present problems forever. He wishes to be able to engage in higher issues from a higher vantage point.

I am working hard toward that blessed time.

Much of my work is the writing of books that will give the benefit of applied ESP systems to the public. There will be a second dream book on areas that I am still researching, such as telepathic dreams and the techniques of gaining higher degrees of consciousness while a dream is in progress so that ESP demands can be made in that state. A second book on card reading is in the making as are books on the following subjects: (1) how to convert Rorschach-type blots to ESP purposes; (2) how to convert geoplasmic effects to ESP purposes; and (3) the role of ESP in answered prayer.

Most of my remaining time is spent with my small research group, the Applied ESP Research Society (A.E.R.S.), in which I direct experiments that supply much of the material for my books. It is amazing, at first thought, that an unfunded lay person can make the progress that I have in leading a group through experiments that evolve into working systems of applied ESP. Yet the very informality of a "laboratory" that is nothing more than a part-time use of my living-dining area is conducive to ESP. In this relaxed atmosphere, my "colleagues" and I—mostly a group of nondegreed people like myself, with only a sprinkling of PhDs, who have sought me out to learn about ESP—conduct some of the most sophisticated experiments in the world. At this point, however, some of our experiments have gone as far as the A.E.R.S. can take them without the funds, grants, and endowments we hope to attract in order to carry on computerized experiments and in order to consult with scientists who specialize in areas to which our various research projects relate.

Readers of this book can cooperate in our research project in the area of dreams—and thus help us fulfill our wish to make this a better world—by sending in reports of results obtained by following the instructions in these pages. All dream reports will be kept strictly confidential in my personal files. For A.E.R.S. study purposes, I will transfer the dream data into a card file system without personal names, and names of persons submitting dreams will not be published without permission. Our contact address for this dream project is P.O. Box 386, Lemon Grove, California 92045.

I shall be especially grateful for case histories in which all or part of the ESP material was interpreted through codes in popular dream books.

It is my wish, one of my most fervent desires, that our parapsychologists shall discover that my code methodologies are the key to ESP for everyone. I do not mean to say our parapsychologists have been remiss in researching the possibilities of an applied ESP via codes. But, in the case of artifacts, they studied only codes that were at hand, such as the ancient I Ching—never my scientifically upgraded codes that can produce highly objective messages. And, in the case of dreams, our parapsychologists did not have the advantage of my method of combining a code with other interpretive techniques, nor did they know how to train the dream faculty to use a code.

Case histories from people in all walks of life will impress our parapsychologists to give my methodologies the research and application that can bring humanity into a higher estate than has ever been known.

Index

1 2 3 4 5 6 7 ← P Y → 9 8 7 6 5 4